Settling Down

FOR MY WIFE AND FAMILY

Settling Down

James Whitaker

A Quartet Publication

First published by Quartet Books Limited 1981

Quartet Books Limited
A member of the Namara Group
27/29 Goodge Street, London W1P 1FD

ISBN 0 7043 3385 6

Printed in Great Britain

Contents

The Background

The announcement was simple and to the point: 'The Princess Elizabeth, Duchess of Edinburgh, was safely delivered of a Prince at 9.14 p.m. today. Her Royal Highness and her son are both doing well.'

Londoners, together with the odd foreigner sensing it was a great occasion and out-of-town revellers, went wild with excitement.

The day was Sunday, 14 November 1948 and Britain's hard-done-by population, with war only recently over, wanted an excuse to celebrate. In those dreary days of continuing austerity they were happy to drink the health of almost anybody. So the fact their beloved King George VI had just been made a grandfather for the first time meant double rejoicing outside the railings of the bomb-damaged Buckingham Palace at the head of The Mall.

The first clue to what had happened came when a royal servant, dressed in blue livery, crossed the gravelled forecourt to the impressive palace gates and started to whisper in the ear of a bobby who was good-naturedly controlling the pressing crowd. The policeman flushed with pleasure, grinned from ear to ear, turned to the now-silent people closest to him and shouted: 'It's a boy!' An enormous cheer went up as the message was relayed from one person to the next and groups started to sing 'For he's a jolly good fellow'. A Welsh contingent, rather more patriotically, chanted 'Land of our Fathers'.

The King and Queen, like Prince Philip, Duke of Edinburgh, waiting inside the Palace, were naturally the first to be informed that their darling daughter, Lilibet, had given birth to a perfect 7 pound 6 ounce son.

Prince Philip, to help kill time, had been playing an energetic game of squash with his secretary and friend, Lieutenant-Commander Michael Parker, when told that the birth was imminent by Sir Alan Lascelles, private secretary to King George VI. Headlong he ran to the Buhl room to find his wife still not conscious after a general anaesthetic after it had been decided by the attending physicians that a forceps delivery was necessary. He waited impatiently at her bedside until he helped to open her eyes with a kiss. And then, excitedly and proudly, he told his still-drowsy wife that she had presented him with a son.

15 December 1948. Four generations of the Royal Family: Queen Mary, King George VI, Princess Elizabeth and the newly christened Charles Philip Arthur George, after the ceremony conducted at Buckingham Palace by the Archbishop of Canterbury.

On Monday morning, less than 12 hours after Charles's birth, office-bound workers pause to read the official announcement posted on the railings outside Buckingham Palace.

Smilingly, she received a bouquet of her favourite carnations and roses and heard how the baby's head had already been toasted in champagne. No other drink seemed appropriate enough, and, whether or not there is any connection, it is this particular alcoholic beverage that has remained Prince Charles's tipple throughout his adult life. This is not forgetting the well-publicized penchant for cherry brandy which got him into trouble when he was a Gordonstoun schoolboy!

News of the birth, officially posted on the palace railings by now, spread thoroughout the West End and, indeed, throughout the world. Telegrams informing everyone of note were dispatched. They had previously been written in readiness. Only the word 'Prince' needed to be filled into the blank space.

The boisterous, happy crowd, still waiting outside the palace although it was well after midnight, was finally persuaded to quieten down so that the exhausted Princess Elizabeth could get some sleep, and eventually went home. Throughout all this, the infant Prince Charles, swathed in his royal-blue clothes, slept on contentedly, oblivious to the fact that, during the very act of his birth, he was creating history.

King George VI, upset at a squabble some twenty years earlier as to which Minister of the Crown should be present at the birth of his younger daughter, Princess Margaret, had decreed that it was totally unnecessary for any member of the Government to attend future royal births. An official Buckingham Palace announcement therefore stated:

The Home Secretary [in 1948 it was Mr Chuter Ede] will not be summoned personally to Buckingham Palace. The attendance of a Minister of the Crown at a birth in the Royal Family is not a statutory requirement or a constitutional necessity.

It is merely the survival of an archaic custom and the King feels that it is unnecessary to continue further a practice for which there is no legal requirement.

The birth of Prince Charles – the first royal child to be born at Buckingham Palace for sixty-two years – was acclaimed with total rapture by the British public. It also ensured continuity of succession to the throne, even though, at this time, Prince Charles was not assured of one day inheriting the title of king. In November 1948, his mother was only heiress presumptive to the crown and Charles was purely heir apparent to the Dukedom of Edinburgh. But in reality only three things could stop him succeeding to the throne in due course: King George VI producing a son, who would have had constitutional preference over both his daughters Elizabeth and Margaret; Prince Charles dying before his mother; or, unlikeliest of all, a revolution with a presidential figure installed as Head of State in place of the Queen.

Today, of course, Prince Charles is heir to the throne, with the Princes Andrew and Edward next in line, followed by Princess Anne. But this state will not last after his Princess of Wales (which is the official title of Lady Diana on marriage) produces children. They will then precede the claims of his brothers and sister.

A continuing argument revolves around whether the Queen will ever step down from her throne in favour of Prince Charles. Some say it could happen when she is sixty (in 1987), others that she will disappear quietly after seeing in the year 2000. I firmly believe it will never happen. And, sad though it may be, I think that the Prince of Wales could be an old-age pensioner before he becomes sovereign.

Royal aides, courtiers and historians have always been adamant that there will never be an abdication. The damage caused to the Royal Family over the circumstances surrounding the abdication of Edward VIII in 1936 is still far too fresh in many people's minds for such an act to take place, if even for the best of reasons.

There were many people at that time (in fact in a poll it was more than 50 per cent of the public) who would happily have let the Royal Family slip into oblivion and gentle retirement. The hard and loving work put in by King George VI and his adored wife (later to become universally known as the Queen Mum) did much to restore the lost prestige caused by the abdication crisis. But, just as important, it is the tradition of 'never deserting the post' that provides the British with so much faith in their Royal Family.

Abdication has no precedent in British constitutional history. The only sovereign ever to step down willingly was King Edward VIII (later Duke of Windsor) so he could marry American double divorcee Wallis Simpson. All other monarchs who went before their natural time either had their heads cut off or were booted out with little ceremony, as happened to James II for refusing to deny his Roman Catholic faith.

One of the greatest assets of the British monarchy is the air of mystique that surrounds it. Try to make its members like mere mortals whom we can compare with others, and much of our respect would disappear. Mr Angus Ogilvy, who married Princess Alexandra in the early 1960s, soon found out what happens if a member of the Royal

Family is treated in too ordinary and explicable a way. Immediately after their marriage in 1963, Mr Ogilvy, now a director of the world-famous auctioneers, Sotheby's, would introduce his pretty young wife to his chums as Alexandra. It didn't happen in hearing of 'outsiders' in public. The informality took place in the privacy of their own home, among the most intimate of Mr Ogilvy's friends. Princess Alexandra certainly didn't object. In fact she thought it was ridiculous that she should be formally addressed as Ma'am (as in 'jam', not Marm as in 'charm',which is purely theatrical)or Your Royal Highness.

But her mother did object. Vehemently. In fact, Princess Marina, Duchess of Kent, was so angry when she heard what was going on that she immediately sent for the hapless Mr Ogilvy.

'Angus!' she ordered him. 'You must not introduce my daughter, your wife, to your friends by her first name. You must keep a distance between Us and Them. There must be this air of mystery. It is the only way we will survive in the way it is now'.

Angus Ogilvy, a charming, polite man who is crippled with arthritis to such an extent that he cries out with pain and can hardly walk at times, regrets that he did not accept the proffered title when he married. This is not for himself at all, since he holds little store by titles, but for the reasons just mentioned. As a result of remaining plain Mr Angus Ogilvy, his children James and Marina have no prefix or title to their names. Not even the exceptionally mundane Hon. This, Mr Ogilvy now concedes, does not set his kids apart from others as much as is necessary to keep the mystique surrounding Royals going.

The same mistake was not allowed by the Queen when her sister Princess Margaret married humble photographer Antony Armstrong-Jones. On 6 May 1960 Tony, much to the amusement of some of his arty bohemian friends, accepted the title of Earl of Snowdon not so much because he wanted it as because his future sister-in-law insisted. And, in these circumstances, *HER* wish is very much anybody else's command. But the result is that their children now have suitably regal titles. Their son David is officially titled Viscount Linley, while their delightful and most attractive daughter is Lady Sarah Armstrong-Jones.

Testing out, not too seriously, the sort of reaction there would be to a suggestion of abdication, the Queen once said in the mid 1960s that it could be wise for her to step down when the day came that Prince Charles might do a better job. She was with the most senior and closest members of her family at Windsor Castle at the time, and they all looked aghast. She assured them she was only joking, and the matter has not been raised seriously since. In fact it is quite clear that the idea of getting older and older in the job rather appeals to the Queen.

Venerability, she realizes, can have enormous pulling power and strength. She noticed with huge pleasure the way the nation rose to the occasion with so much love and affection when her mother, the Queen Mother, celebrated her eightieth birthday in August 1980. And she is not unaware of the enormous esteem in which her great-great-grandmother Queen Victoria was held – particularly in the latter years of her life, when she came back to her people after the years of being a virtual recluse following the death of her adored Prince Albert. Indeed, the Queen readily accepts that the last few years of Queen Victoria's life were the most popular of her reign.

Prince Charles himself has, in fact, repeatedly said that the Queen will never abdicate. He has even gone on record publicly as saying it won't ever happen, and I think this should be believed. Company chairmen retire, prime ministers step down in favour of younger, more vigorous successors, electricians, carpenters and garage mechanics all allow themselves to be pensioned off. But they are mere mortals. Kings and Queens must not be seen to be the same. It would be another erosion of the air of mystery which is so necessary, indeed vital, to the idea of monarchy.

After a totally traditional upbringing as a baby – with the usual retinue of nannies, servants fussing too much, and seeing far too little of his mother because of the amount of work she suddenly had as a result of King George VI dying when Prince Charles was barely aged three – plans were formulated as to which direction his life should take.

It was at this time in the early 1950s that the power, wisdom and single-mindedness of Prince Philip first became obvious to court officials. The Duke of Edinburgh is emphatically not a figurehead who trails around with the Queen every now and then, making suitable remarks (or often, in his case, unsuitable remarks). Quietly, and with enormous discretion and little tub-thumping, he is very much a power behind the throne. No major decision is ever taken by the Queen without first seeking her husband's advice and approval.

In fact, in many ways, he is more powerful than she is. Constitutionally, the sovereign has no power at all, only what we, through Parliament, are prepared to grant. But Prince Philip is a very forceful personality and can persuade the Queen what should be done.

Happily for us all, Prince Philip is a wise and clever person who has guided his wife most successfully all their married life. And it was very much Philip who decided what should happen to their son and heir. The first thing he insisted upon was that Prince Charles should be removed from the excessive petticoat power provided by the female staff who predominantly looked after him at Sandringham, Windsor and Buckingham Palace.

By now nearly two years old, Charles watches the State Opening of Parliament under the watchful eyes of two nannies. Prince Philip made strenuous efforts to wean him away from this 'petticoat power'.

Prince Philip was concerned about other things, too. He worried that his young son was a class of just one when being taught the three 'Rs' by his first governess, Katharine Peebles. Miss Peebles, affectionately known as Mispy, later recalled some of the problems of being in not-so-splendid isolation. She said 'if you raised your voice to him, he would draw back into his shell and for a time you would be able to do nothing with him. He liked being amused rather than amusing himself.'

The Royals' favourite nanny, Miss Mabel Anderson, another Scotswoman, like Miss Peebles, who has only just left looking after Princess Anne's first child, Peter Phillips, agreed there was a problem. She said at the time: 'He was never as boisterous or as noisy as Princess Anne. She had a much stronger, more extrovert personality. She didn't exactly push him aside, but she certainly was a more forceful child'.

Left: 'He was never as boisterous or as noisy as Princess Anne. She had a much stronger, more extrovert personality.' Charles petulantly ignores events on the field at Windsor Great Park in 1952.

Right: A rare shopping expedition for the young Prince. Clutching a parcel containing a toy he has just bought, Charles leaves a shop in Ballater in the company of Lady Mary Cook and her mother, Lady Leicester. Handling money was an unusual experience for him.

And then Prince Philip was worried about other little problems. Prince Charles, in his closeted early childhood, didn't know the difference between ordinary coins such as a half-crown (now 12½p) or a florin (10p). He didn't know how to mix with other children easily. He never stood in queues on a Saturday morning to buy himself an ice cream.

The situation simply couldn't arise. He didn't handle money. If he wanted something, Nanny would produce the necessary amount.

Above: In his boyhood, Charles was surrounded by reflections of himself in more ways than one. Constantly played up to, he never formed the easy, natural friendships that other boys did. This left him with an inbuilt shyness, a lack of self-confidence which, even now, manifests itself in nervous, obsessive gestures (facing page).

It all generated a lack of self-confidence, a shy growing awareness that he really was different from other children. Although he did have suitable friends, drawn from a limited circle of royally approved and tested families, they just couldn't match the splendour and grandeur in which he was growing up.

Royal servants from the humble to the mighty addressed the Prince simply as Charles (and continued to do so until his eighteenth birthday), but he had so many more around him than any of his chums. This made him feel awkward and embarrassed and pushed him into his shell even further.

There is little question but that the Prince has suffered all his life from a lack of confidence. It may seem incredible in such a person but watch him closely when is is on public display and the signs are there. He continually plays with the gold signet ring on his left hand. He clasps and unclasps his hands rapidly, placing them behind his back one minute and in the pocket to his jacket the next. He frequently puts his left hand to the bridge of his nose, and all the time he moistens his lips nervously.

There are also days when his jaw develops a nervous tic and his skin often seems far from the peaches-and-cream complexion normally associated with members of the Royal Family. But recently, and especially since the announcement of his engagement to Lady Diana Spencer, there has been a definite improvement in his approach to the business of mixing and conversing with people. As a result, he has endeared himself to the general public better than ever previously. There has never been any question of his shirking his duty in the past. But there were so many occasions when he looked decidedly uncomfortable while carrying out official engagements. It was obvious he was having to make a determined effort.

On his recent tour 'down under', which came just a few weeks after his engagement, he was the most relaxed I have ever seen him on his brilliantly successful 'walkabouts'. He actually looked as if he was enjoying meeting the many thousands who turned out to greet him wherever he went. Previously, such events had obviously been a bit of an ordeal for him. You could see he was hardly taking in anything being said to him, so intent was he on worrying what he would say to the next person he'd meet. But in New Zealand, where on some days he did as many as three 'walkabouts' apart from other duties, he was very much more relaxed. As a result, he became almost a headache to his hosts as he overran engagement after engagement in his quest to meet the entire population.

Lady Diana Spencer was the name on everybody's lips as he moved from one side of the cordoned-off road to the other, and you could sense the happiness and pride in his voice as he gently explained to them how much he would have liked Diana to be with him during his visit. There was such disappointment that she wasn't there.

'But', the Prince kept saying, 'I will be back again and then she will be at my side. I would love to show her off to you and I know she would enjoy all this as much as I do'.

The point of all this is that, at long last, the Prince had somebody else to worry about and talk about. He could forget his own problems and could publicly express his hopes, aspirations and plans for the woman who was to be his partner for life. In so doing, the Prince's shyness and nervousness became markedly less noticeable. It is interesting that, despite everything done for the Prince during the whole of his life, it took the gentleness of Lady Diana to give Prince Charles the final coating of confidence that he needed.

Prince Philip's early plan to remove Charles from the sanctity of Buckingham Palace, a governess and the resultant privacy, and to send him to a school with ordinary (or reasonably ordinary) children, was sensational. No child of a sovereign had ever been publicly educated before. But the bold plan did have its problems. Among them was the behaviour of the media, which has been a recurring theme all Charles's life.

Naturally enough, there was enormous interest in the decision to send the Prince to Hill House School in Knightsbridge, and they besieged the place on his first day there. And, indeed, on several succeeding days.

Prince Charles knows that newspapers, television, magazines and cameramen want to photograph and record almost everything he does

Even when Charles retreats from the spotlight, vigilant media men remain alert to record his every move. A few minutes' welcome rest snatched between polo games at Cowdray Park.

all the time, and he expects this sort of attention and knows how to deal with it. In fact, he once told me: 'The day that this doesn't happen is the day I have to worry'. But, in 1956, he was very uncertain, very unsure of himself and nervous of the unexpected. The Queen, rather naively, was shocked at the attention. She had asked the Hill House Headmaster, Colonel Henry Townsend, that her son be treated like any other pupil. And instead there was chaos, confusion and fighting going on outside the school front door.

The first of many appeals went out to Fleet Street editors.

'Please give him a chance', begged the Queen. 'Let him settle down'.

The situation did improve marginally, but the intense interest continued and has not eased off to this day.

At all events, the breach had been made and Prince Charles remained at his first school for two terms, despite missing most of the second one when he had his tonsils out. His school report was adequate and both his parents considered, all in all, that their daring departure from the status quo had been a success.

The only area that the Prince could not come to grips with was an understanding of maths. His report on this subject said: 'Below form average. Careful but slow. Not very keen'. But that was all right and was purely following in a family tradition. The Queen has always been lousy at mathematics and has hardly suffered as a result. And it is exactly the same with Lady Diana. She loathes maths, she says.

Prince Philip's attitude to reports is sensible and practical. He has said to all his children: 'Look, I'm only going to bother if you are permanently at the bottom. I really couldn't care less where you are. Just stay in the middle, that's all I ask'.

The next school chosen for Prince Charles was Cheam, one of the country's leading preparatory schools in Berkshire. Once again, it was the insistence of Prince Philip that got him there. The Queen certainly didn't object, but she was still nervous at this revolutionary method of educating the heir to the throne and she was also concerned about the continuing interest from newspapers and television.

But Cheam was a good school that Prince Philip knew particularly well. He himself was educated there. It is a boarding school, so it meant that, for the first time, the young Prince Charles would be living away from the comforts of the royal homes.

'Good for him', insisted his father. 'It will teach him to stand on his own two feet'.

Nobody really argued against this logic. 'What a good idea', agreed everybody who makes up the tiny circle of friends who surround the Royal Family.

The only person who didn't like what happened from now on and for the next ten years or so was Prince Charles himself. Basically, the young Prince hated school, both at Cheam and subsequently at Gordonstoun, again a school at which Prince Philip had been educated.

Young boys, and their mothers in particular, soon learn to live with the separation that boarding school brings. Usually the settling down period is a fortnight or three weeks. This was not to be the case with Prince Charles. It has been said since that it took the Prince five years to settle down at Cheam, and on the day when he finally did, it was time to leave.

He didn't find it easy to mix with other boys, who were quite cruel to him, on occasions teasing him about being who he was. He didn't take to team games (to this day he still prefers the sports where he relies on his own skills). He was awkward and shy. And he was homesick.

The bed on which he slept was hard, there were ninety-nine almost totally strange faces to get to know, and for the first time in his life he had to do strange things like make his own bed and clean out the dormitory.

There was a great deal of soul-searching by the Queen and Prince Philip when it began to dawn on them that this revolutionary plan wasn't working terribly well. One member of the school staff described the Prince as 'Shy, nervous, sullen, sometimes precocious'. Another went on: 'He never settled in with the rest of the school at any time until the last few weeks of his final term. But at least we got him prepared for the next stage of his life and I suppose this is all we were really meant to do'.

One thing that didn't help Prince Charles during this unhappy period of his life was the announcement by the Queen that her son was to be created Prince of Wales. It happened during the summer term of 1958 after the Prince had been at the school nearly one year. The proclamation came at the conclusion of the Commonwealth Games then taking place in Cardiff.

The Prince and a few of his friends were watching the event on the television set of the headmaster, Peter Beck, when he heard his mother say: 'I want to take this opportunity of speaking to all Welsh people not only in this area, but wherever they may be'.

The boys weren't terribly interested in what was being said until the Queen announced, out of the blue: 'I intend to create my son Charles Prince of Wales today'.

When the applause died down, the Queen went on: 'When he is grown up I will present him to you at Caernarvon'.

The timing of the announcement is now generally considered to have been a mistake. The Queen herself has said privately that she regrets the way it was done. The Prince himself later recalled his vivid memory of that moment despite knowing what was about to happen. He has said: 'I remember being acutely embarrassed when it was announced. I heard this marvellous great cheer coming from the stadium in Cardiff, and I think for a little boy of nine it was rather bewildering. All the others turned and looked at me in amazement'.

It served purely to highlight the impossibility of the Queen's great desire for her son to be treated the same way as any other boy in the school. All it did was to set him even further apart.

This has been a problem for the Prince all his life, and will continue to be one until the day he dies. However much he may argue that to the contrary, merely because of who he is, he simply doesn't have any idea how everybody else lives. Or what they are like.

Time after time I have watched people I know quite well become totally unrecognizable as soon as the Prince is with them. As he walks into a room, the first noticeable thing is the way its occupants straighten up and begin to smile. There is nothing natural in the way they then start to behave whenever the Prince is anywhere near them. Dignitaries, politicians and even people like former jockey Brough Scott, now a sports writer with the *Sunday Times* and a television racing commentator, adopt, without even realizing it, a slightly silly expression.

Brough, a cheerful self-confident type of person, who is normally at ease with everybody, met the Prince at Sandown Park in March 1981 just before the Prince rode his steeplechaser Good Prospect in a race. It was hard to recognize Brough. His grin wasn't natural, he laughed too much as he was waiting to be introduced to the Prince at the final fence, and he wasn't the same person he had been an hour before.

But this is par for the course. The Prince never meets the person unless he is in constant communication with them or the person is a close friend of many years' standing. His aides protest that this is not the case. They claim that, after about twenty minutes of chatting, the person relaxes enough to be his usual self.

The problem with this argument is that the Prince seldom has the chance to spend even as little time as this talking to one person. And, from my experience of watching close friends of HRH, as he is known by many of those who surround him, sufficient relaxation rarely happens.

There are exceptions. An easy relationship that obviously exists between the Prince and Charles Palmer-Tomkinson, who acts as his host in Klosters for his annual skiing holiday in Switzerland in January each year. Others who behave as themselves in his company include his polo manager, the charming and urbane Major Ronnie Ferguson, and his former polo coach, the no-frills, no-fuss, Sinclair Hill, who is in true Aussie style in awe of nobody. And there is his old trusted friend Nick Soames, son of our former Ambassador to Paris, Lord Soames.

Close friend Charles Palmer-Tomkinson and bodyguard John MacLean frog-march Prince Charles across the slippery ice at Klosters. Few are afforded such spontaneous, intimate contact with the Prince.

Those who would like to think they are natural in his presence but who are not are numerous. They include his polo-playing chum, Lord 'Sam' Vestey, the multi-millionaire meat and shipping baron; his racehorse trainer, Nick Gaselee; the chairman of the Guards Polo Club at Windsor, Gerard Leigh; and his old salmon-fishing pal, Lord Tryon, the husband of his favourite married woman, Lady 'Dale' Tryon, whom he affectionately calls Kanga.

It is hardly a big problem for any of them when they are in the presence of the Prince. But one thing they are not: natural. And yet they are like everybody else who ever has contact with HRH on either a brief, one-off introduction or on a much more permanent basis.

The Prince would not accept this readily. But how often does he get told the truth? When he is out and about he will be steered away from any sort of controversy where he is likely to be told what's what. The police make sure demonstrators are kept well away from him.

To his credit, the Prince often does not approve of this and will try to get to the protestors to ask for himself what they are trying to say. But, even then, he is unlikely to get real answers. People tend to crumble as soon as they get near him. Not long ago half a dozen punk rockers at Windsor Park were watching him play a game of polo. At the end, somewhat nervously, they approached the Prince, who was busy changing, to invite him to a concert about to be given by a punk group.

Charles in deep discussion with his racehorse trainer, Nick Gaselee, at Sandown Park. Their empathy contrasts with the mutual incomprehension evident in the chance meeting with a group of punks (below).

The Prince, his detective watching anxiously, looked them straight in the eyes and cracked a joke about whether their outrageously pink and orange coloured hair had been hired from the wig shop. At once the group started to act silly. They mainly giggled nervously, they started to shuffle around, not looking at the Prince as they talked to him. Once again, Prince Charles was not speaking to any real person.

But the position and title of the Prince of Wales is a formidable one. Nobody says 'No you can't do that', to Prince Charles. Neither do they say: 'You can't go there, I am afraid to tell you'. When he arrives somewhere, the road is clean and the paint invariably new. (He once commented: 'I hate the smell of new paint. It sticks in my nose and makes me feel nauseous. Why do people paint everything when I am due somewhere?')

And the Prince of Wales doesn't wait in queues. Except nowadays at the bottom of the ski lift in Klosters, Switzerland, after Germans complained two years ago that their tickets were far too expensive for Prince Charles to push in front of them. It came as a surprise and a shock to the Prince when he heard that other skiers had complained about the queue jumping by himself, the Prince and Princess Richard, Duke and Duchess of Gloucester, as well as other members of their skiing party. To his credit, he immediately said that of course he should wait in line with everybody else. But the point is, it hadn't crossed his mind that there could be a complaint. Protocol says that the Prince of Wales goes first – in front of women, even of his own Princess of Wales.

There are few obstacles in the path of royal privilege, but here Charles disentangles himself from a collision with the then Miss Switzerland, Barbara Mayer, on the slopes at Davos.

Tradition and, of course, good manners dictate that, when he arrives anywhere, either privately or officially, everything is spotless. He has never had to walk into a room and start straightening the place up. He doesn't have to shine his own shoes, wash his shirts or underpants or put a crease in his trousers. And HRH doesn't have just one valet to do all this. He has two of them. But would we like it to be any other way? I certainly wouldn't. I don't want the Prince of Wales to be anything like other people.

But it should be realized that he is very different and therefore must find it hard to understand normal problems.

Even when he arrives at the opera at Covent Garden or walks down Queen Street in Auckland, New Zealand, months and months of preparation and thousands of man-hours will have been put into a situation that might not last much over half and hour.

And next time you go to have a look at HRH on a walkabout, for example, take a look up at the roof-tops. Strategically placed along the route you will see good-looking, well-built men with slightly bulging suits. They will be speaking quietly into hand-held walkie-talkies. They will never stop moving and their eyes will never be still. Occasionally they will lift their binoculars to have a closer look at somebody.

That is the sort of security that surrounds the Prince these days. But, in addition, there is one man who will never be more than a few feet from his side at all times. He will be the personal bodyguard assigned to look after HRH.

Prince Charles now has three permanent bodyguards who attend him constantly on a rota basis. Two are superintendants (recently promoted) and one is a sergeant. But, since the assassination of Earl Mountbatten in August 1979, even this sort of cover is considered not nearly sufficient. More than a dozen 'back-up' detectives now work hand in hand with the three main bodyguards. All are supplied by the Metropolitan Police from Scotland Yard (Special Branch men are not used because their job is of a political nature) and all are armed.

There is a very real fear among the people who protect Prince Charles that he could be on the list of a would-be assassin. Following the violent death of Prince Charles's beloved Great-Uncle Dickie when he was blown up on a fishing boat in Ireland, Buckingham Palace received a message. A voice said: 'That is one of the bastards we have got rid of. But we are not resting there. We will get another one soon. And it will be one of the senior members of the family'.

Crank messages are received all the time, but there was something special about this one. I know they believed what was said and the precautions then started to be increased dramatically.

More detectives are being drafted in by the week, and now, of course, there is also Lady Diana to be considered. On the day of the engagement announcement in February, she was given one of Prince Charles's bodyguards at the precise hour of eleven o'clock when the news was made public.

What happened on 5 May 1981 - when a letter bomb addressed to Prince Charles at Buckingham Palace was intercepted and successfully defused – was a chilling reminder of the danger he now walks in constantly. It was the closest any terrorist had ever got to an immediate relative of the Queen and a Buckingham Palace spokeman went so far as to admit that there was 'concern at the threat'. The man chosen to guard Lady Diana for the first few days was Chief Inspector (now Superintendent) Paul Officer, the detective who once helped to save the

Paul Officer, who has been with Prince Charles through thick and thin for more than a decade.

Prince from serious injury – or even worse – on the one occasion when he was physically attacked.

It happened in April 1974, when the Prince was taking a course in underwater warfare at Portland, Dorset. At the time he was a Lieutenant serving aboard the freighter, HMS *Jupiter*.

In the middle of the night he was attacked by a maniac, wielding a chair and a knife, who had disturbed the sleeping Prince just after 2 a.m. After hearing a noise, the Prince had got up and gone to investigate. He was pounced upon for his troubles. The Prince and the attacker, who turned out be to another Lieutenant with a history of mental disorder, were struggling desperately when Paul Officer rushed in to help. Between them, they overpowered the assailant, who has since been committed to a psychiatric hospital indefinitely.

It was also Paul Officer, a 6 foot 3 inch former public schoolboy, who was with the Prince when he collapsed from heat exhaustion in Florida in April 1980 at the end of a hectic game of polo played in extemely humid conditions. Towards the end of the game, Paul watched in horror as the Prince slumped in a buggy, clearly struggling to breathe properly. The entourage around the Prince loosened his collar, fussed around him, but then began to relax their vigil as the Prince continued to assure them he was all right.

The plain-clothes detectives who act as Charles's bodyguards are never more than a few steps away from him at any time. They must also dress to suit the occasion: here, a formal wedding at which HRH was a guest.

But he wasn't. The paramedics and ambulancemen who were watching what was going on knew he wasn't. It was at this stage that a complete misunderstanding happened which was very nearly fatal for the Prince. Somebody – it has never been established exactly who – refused to let the highly trained medics on to the polo field to tend him.

One technique these men would have used on the heir to the throne would have been to place packs of ice around the scrotum. The Prince's temperature needed to be brought down, and this is the best way to do it. But it was hardly a dignified process!

Half-hearted treatment continued until the Prince was put in an open-topped car and started to be taken to the home of American millionaire property man, Bill Ylvisaker, who was the Prince's host for the weekend. During the short journey it was realized that HRH was in a much more serious way than anybody had been prepared to admit. The order was given. 'To the Good Samaritan Hospital, and quick'.

It was never revealed at the time – and there have been denials since, as always happens with scare stories surrounding the Prince – but there then began two dreadful hours which involved real fear for the heir apparent's life. The worst moments came during the thundering ride towards the West Palm Beach hospital, which ironically had once tended the previous Prince of Wales when he was Duke of Windsor. With the Prince and Paul Officer in the car were 'an absolutely terrified' Ronnie Ferguson, the Prince's friend and polo manager, and his equerry, the delightful ex-Foreign Office diplomat Oliver Everett, who, in April, became secretary and personal assistant to Lady Diana.

I have since been told that, during that twenty-five mile journey, which was covered in an incredible twenty minutes, the Prince's heart beat was only just above zero. At one stage nobody could find any pulse at all. The occupants really believed that the Prince was close to death. And the situation was made no better when the Prince is said to have croaked to Everett: 'Don't leave me, Oliver. I think I am dying'.

The driver, becoming increasingly aware of the urgency and drama of the situation, started to drive like a man possessed. He went through red lights, in and out of the busy rush-hour traffic like a dodgem-car driver, and even, on two occasions, drove up on to the pavement to get through. Two American police outriders on motor-cycles could not keep up with the driver of the Prince's car, such was the desperation. At the hospital, there was a stretcher waiting and the Prince, who had 'become the colour of alabaster', was rushed inside.

Controlled panic had been taking place there as hospital staff prepared for the most important vistor they had ever received. A special emergency room was set up as senior doctors were hauled in from their dinner tables to stand by. The Queen was informed, despite it being the middle of the night in England, and a hot line was kept open.

Paul Officer, blond and today almost anorexically thin after losing around four stone in weight during the last two or three years, would never want to go through all that again. In the end, the Prince was released after a good night's rest, having been put on a saline drip while he slept. Poker-faced, the royal party left late the following morning, with the Prince at the wheel of an open-top car (and stupidly not wearing a hat). Discreetly none of the royal aides will discuss that night, but I have had it confirmed that those closest to HRH were subsequently told he was only a hairsbreadth from dying. His super-fitness helped to pull him through.

Detectives who look after the Prince pay a heavy price for a handsome pay packet and what are often long and boring hours. Their job is as demanding as it is unpredictable. They have had to rearrange their own private plans more often than any of them care to think about. And they have sacrificed a lot.

Paul Officer's marriage ended in divorce from his wife Jill two years ago, after spending far too long away from her. He said at the time 'I don't blame anybody, but being away from home so much has made marriage very difficult'.

The other chief inspector looking after the Prince (who was made up to superintendent at the same time as Paul) is a tough, uncompromising Scotsman, John MacLean. He has deliberately forsaken having children to guard 'the boss', as he calls the Prince. He does not believe that his life style is conducive to such ties as kids. The third 'shadow', cool, calm, unflappable fellow Scotsman, Sergeant Jim McMaster, who has only recently become a permanent feature in the life of the Prince, is a bachelor.

His role will soon become even more demanding. Paul Officer is to leave the Prince this autumn, so creating a fairly large gap in the protection squad. Paul will have been with the Prince for more than twelve years (he and John joined at the end of the Prince's university career), but he wants to move on now, believing that the boss's wedding is a good breaking-off point.

But, to return to Prince Charles's school days. After Cheam, the Prince progressed on to Gordonstoun, the tough outward-bound style

Smiles all round – except for Charles – as Prince Philip delivers his son into the hands of Robert Chew, headmaster of Godonstoun. The mood seems to have stayed with Charles for most of his time there.

school founded by Kurt Hahn. The theory of the place, situated in a bleak part of North-East Scotland near Elgin, is that the pupil is taught self-reliance and self-confidence.

Prince Philip had been at school there, and it was he, once again, who asserted his will in ensuring that this was the place chosen to complete his eldest son's schooling. In retrospect, I suppose it was a good idea to send him there, but at the time the Prince went through much doubt and misery.

He began, or, to quote the Prince's own words, 'became incarcerated' at his house, Windmill Lodge, one windy wet day at the end of April 1962. As at Cheam, the Queen implored everybody – from Fleet Street to the headmater Robert Chew – to treat the Prince 'like any other boy'. And, as happened at Cheam, the request was only partially respected. But an advantage of Gordonstoun was that the place was far less accessible to over-nosey journalists.

The Prince was soon introduced to the spartan ways of the school. These included early-morning runs and cold showers; the occasional responsibility of cleaning his dormitory; helping to empty dustbins; and even weeding, and waiting at table on the other boys. It was the one time of his life when HRH lived vaguely like a mere mortal. And he clearly didn't greatly enjoy certain aspects of the situation. I haven't heard of him washing too many dishes since those days.

After the rigours of each day, it was not too surprising that lights went out at 9 p.m. One old boy has since told me, 'That might seem a little bit early, but I can tell you we were all exhausted by this time and more than happy to go to sleep'.

Fagging doesn't exist at Gordonstoun as one of the ideas behoved by the school is that all chores should be done 'for the good of the community'. Prince Charles has since told friends that, for his first few years there, he was 'rather unhappy', and then, later on, 'rather bored' by the place. It will be extremely interesting to see what he and Lady Diana do when their eldest son starts to be educated.

Possibly Prince Charles's biggest problem in relation to Gordonstoun was that, while the school admirably suited the extrovert nature of Prince Philip, his own introvert character gave him huge problems at times. As he confided once: 'I have very little taste for group activities and no great liking for team games like rugger or cricket'.

He also found it difficult to make friends. It has been a problem for him ever since. It is hard to imagine that anybody knows more people than the Prince, but very few have become really close over the years. Being the Prince of Wales has made it all the more difficult for him. As he commented on his early days at Gordonstoun: 'The trouble is that very often the worst people come up first and the really nice ones hang back because they don't want to be accused of sucking up'.

But at this time the Prince did have one very good friend on whom he could rely. He was Norton Knatchbull, grandson of Lord Louis Mountbatten. Since the earl was assassinated by Irish terrorists on August Bank Holiday Monday in 1979, Norton has inherited the courtesy title of Lord Romsey.

Whether the Prince and Norton are as pally as many once thought is open to question these days. At one time it was widely believed in court circles that Norton was destined to become the Prince's closest adviser, confidant and friend. There seemed every chance that he might even give up a film-making career to devote his life to serving the Prince.

Norton Knatchbull arriving for his Romsey Abbey wedding escorted by his best man. The two have not always been so closely in step in recent years.

It hasn't happened, and in fact the two, who are of similar age, have seen little of each other recently. The Prince did act as best man at the Romsey Abbey wedding of Norton and Penny Eastwood, but there has been a steady drifting apart of the Royal Family and Norton's family since the death of Mountbatten.

The Queen never approved of the amount of influence that 'Dickie' seemed to have over Prince Charles, and she had enormous reservations over the way Mountbatten pushed the suitability of Lady Amanda Knatchbull (Norton's younger sister) as a bride for Prince Charles.

Some members of the Royal Family were happier than others in the company of Lord Mountbatten: Prince Charles, Princess Michael of Kent, the Queen and 'Dickie' watching polo at Smith's Lawn, Windsor.

A further rift between the Royal Family and the Brabournes was caused when it was revealed that the award-winning writer and acclaimed naval historian Richard Hough was to be first off the mark with a biography of Lord Mountbatten in August 1980. Lord Brabourne complained bitterly, and said he was 'surprised' by a number of Hough's claims about his murdered father-in-law.

In a stinging letter to the *Bookseller*, the influential organ of the book trade, Lord Brabourne wrote: 'Mr Hough states his biography is the book Mountbatten wanted me (Hough) to write. It surprises me greatly as it does all relations and close friends of Lord Mountbatten to whom I have spoken, that my father-in-law had any wish that Mr Hough should undertake "an informal biography".'

The root of the trouble was that Brabourne's family had commissioned an official work from the Old Etonian writer and publisher, Philip Ziegler, who was expecting to make 'more than £100,000' from it. It was felt Hough's book might seriously dent this figure.

I was told at the time that the Queen was 'very unhappy' at this 'unseemly public squabbling' over who was making how much. She is said to have commented 'I find the whole business most distasteful'.

Prince Charles's disillusionment with things Mountbatten became even more obvious when he failed to attend the charity premiere of the film *The Mirror Crack'd* in March 1981, just after he had become engaged. All money raised from that evening was to go to the Mountbatten Memorial Trust, of which Prince Charles is chairman.

He could, so easily, have 'launched' Lady Diana that night. The resultant publicity would have boosted trust funds and given the whole project a much-needed fillip. The Prince – and, of course, Lady Diana – stayed away from the event, and, instead, delayed their public debut together in favour of an evening in aid of the Royal Opera Appeal, which has been most successful and didn't need any particular 'help'.

Buckingham Palace and the Mountbatten Memorial Trust organizers were not keen to discuss what was going on. A trust spokesman said carefully: 'We don't know what he will be doing for us. We shall fit him in where he is able to help us'. Sixteen months after being set up the Memorial Trust had raised only a paltry £500,000 – half of which came from two individual donations. In charity terms, this was considered to be a poor sort of response.

It is said today that the Mountbatten influence is gone for ever – much to the relief of all the senior Buckingham Palace officials. The final nail in the Knatchbull coffin came when the engagement to Lady Diana was announced.

Earl Mountbatten had unashamedly promoted Lady Amanda as the person who should become the Princess of Wales. In an off-the-record interview with an American weekly magazine of enormous influence, he once more or less guaranteed that Amanda would be the one. He in fact used journalists of power to promote his granddaughter. The *Daily Express*'s famous columnist, Jean Rook, believed what she was being told. So did Prince Charles's biographer, Tony Holden, who wrote a superb and best-selling book on the Prince of Wales in 1979.

Tony was so convinced that Prince Charles's future wife would be Amanda that one night in Fleet Street's famous El Vino wine bar he started to bet fairly large sums of money on what he believed. William Hickey, the gossip columnist, Christopher Wilson and myself accommodated him with few qualms. We may even get paid soon!

‘It’s not as easy as it looks’. Evidently Charles has taken a lump out of the bread board before finding the target.

It was during the Prince’s time at Gordonstoun that one of the great watersheds of his life occurred. The decision was taken for the Prince to spend two terms at Timbertops in Australia, the outback section of Geelong Grammar School. It was the first visit of a Prince of Wales to Australia for forty-five years and, as usual, the Prince was full of apprehension. It was also his first visit abroad without one or other of his parents.

He did, however, have with him the then equerry to Prince Philip, Squadron Leader David Checketts, a man who was to become a major influence in Prince Charles’s life. Squadron Leader Checketts, now Sir David Checketts, guided the Prince through his formative years with skill, understanding and compassion. He later became the Prince’s first private secretary. In Australia, Checketts acted as advisor and substitute father-figure to the still very unsure Charles, who started at Timbertop as a shy, rather young seventeen-year-old in January 1966.

By the end of this experimental schooling period, Checketts was saying: ‘I went out there with a boy and returned with a man’. The Prince himself has admitted that, during the seven months he was there, he grew from being a child into the early stages of manhood. ‘Australia got me over my shyness’, he has said.

On his return to Gordonstoun, the Prince became ‘Helper’ head of his house, and then, the next term, was given the greatest accolade of all when he was chosen as Guardian, the title given to the head boy of the school. Prince Philip was particularly proud of this. He had held the same position when he was there, and it seemed the final justification for having sent his son to this particular establishment.

Having passed his ‘A’-levels in French and history, the Prince was also qualified to go on to university. Many other students struggling to get a place in any university, let alone Trinity College, Cambridge, complained at what they considered favouritism. To his horror, he was

THE
CAMBRIDG
PAD

Charles studying in his rooms and at a tutorial
His style of dress sets him somewhat apart
from other students, though he seems to have adopted
the popular habit of wearing odd socks.

even named in a motion discussed at the annual conference of the National Union of Students, Swansea University College, and Goldsmiths' College, London. It sarcastically congratulated the Prince on his recent 'exceptional performance' in the GCE examination and on his 'rare good fortune' in obtaining a place at Cambridge University with just two 'A'-Levels.

But the Prince persevered, studied anthropology and archaeology to begin with before changing to history, after consultations with the Master of Trinity, former cabinet Minster, Lord ('Rab') Butler, and came away with an 'average' degree. This was in June 1970, and was achieved despite a nine-week leave of absence when the Prince interrupted his studies to attend the University College of Wales, Aberystwyth.

Flying lesson in an RAF Chipmunk trainer at Tangmere.

As Prince of Wales, it was felt advisable that he should do this, and he impressed many people with his diligence. He even learned a reasonable amount of Welsh, which was put to the test when he addressed the Welsh League of Youth in their own language. He had 300 words to utter, and he did so, to wide applause, without making a single mistake. Two and a half months later, the Prince had a further triumph at Caernarvon Castle, when he was officially invested as Prince of Wales in a magnificent ceremony watched by a television audience of 500 million around the world.

Prince Charles was growing up fast. His character was gaining an identity of its own and the next stage was a services career. There was never any real doubt that he would end up in the Senior Service. The Prince's ancestors from time immemorial went into the navy as part of their education. But, to begin with, the Prince had a spell in the Royal Air Force, joining the RAF College, Cranwell, in March 1971 as a flight lieutenant. His code name was Golden Eagle. He already knew how to fly, having learned at Cambridge on a twin-engined Eagle Basset.

At Cranwell he was taught advanced flying on the 440 m.p.h. Jet Provost. Like everything else he has attempted in life, the Prince made a success of what he was doing, and it came as no surprise when, a few months later, he was presented with his pilot's wings. It was at this time that the Prince made his first parachute jump and showed to the world the sort of guts he possesses. His nickname of 'Action Man' is something he hates. But really he is very aptly so described. It was Peter Tory, the *Daily Express* gossip columnist, who gave him this label after chronicling his daring exploits while wearing so many different and fancy outfits.

Often frustrated by his sometimes restrictive role in life, the Prince has always tempted the fates. Apart from being the first Prince of Wales in history to gain a university degree, he has captained his own ship, led a Young England polo team in combat against the old enemies the French, flown both jets and helicopters, trained as a frogman and a commando and attempted to jump round Sandown and Cheltenham on his own race horse.

One of the Prince's greatest faults is his inability to take criticism. Twice I have seen him react angrily when meeting reporters who have passed uncomplimentary comments about his skills or character. Following a fall from his horse Good Prospect at the 1981 Cheltenham National Hunt Festival meeting, there were many articles concerning his ability to compete at such a high level. 'Absolute twaddle', was the Prince's reply. He went on: 'Too many comments are being made by people who don't know what they are talking about'.

But this is not true. Several experts at the sport thought the Prince behaved ridiculously in competing in the Kim Muir chase at Cheltenham. This is the top race for amateurs in the country, and he was out of his class . In the end he literally fell off his horse just as he had done a few days earlier at Sandown.

Running across Smith's Lawn, Windsor.

Ladbroke's man, Mike Dillon, got it right when he said: 'He came off because he was knackered'. But the worst aspect was that the highly professional crowd of racegoers simply laughed at HRH when it happened for a second time. It was all right to fool around at a meeting like the Grand Military at Sandown, they thought, but Cheltenham was for hard-bitten professionals and there was no room for amateurs, even if they were princes of the realm. Prince Charles struck out at the ground with his whip in sheer frustration as he rolled over at Cheltenham, knowing he looked foolish.

After the fall. Good Prospect and his crestfallen rider return to the unsaddling enclosure

I have spoken to the Prince about why he rode in races of this standard rather than in a far less competitive point-to-point. 'My trainer, Mr (Nick) Gaselee has said it is safer for me to compete against the top amateurs rather than against unpredictable and therefore much more dangerous point-to-point riders', replied the Prince. But many remain unconvinced by this argument and think, at this stage of his riding career, that he would be better off learning the business at a much lower grade.

During his recent tour of Australia, the Prince said: 'It is my greatest ambition to ride in the Grand National at Liverpool. It is the single most exciting thing I could ever hope to do'. A terrifying prospect, but typical of his bravery. Happily, he is not allowed to compete in this particular race until he has had fifteen rides in public.

During the same trip 'down under' the Prince showed his irritability at comments that one of his biggest faults was his tardiness at dealing with official papers given him to read, digest and subsequently sign. 'Not true and not fair' was his comment. And yet it is well known by the officials who surround him at the palace that he is very slow at returning documents. Paperwork bores him.

One thing for which I have great sympathy for the Prince is the way he can attempt almost nothing in privacy. It is most unnerving for

'He can attempt almost nothing in privacy'. The attentions of the media are a major irritation for the Prince.

him that, when a dozen like-minded people line up to do something, the public should be interested in only one of the competitors. Like other members of the Royal Family, Prince Charles is much more at home with the outdoor life and therefore can be easily watched by so-called rubber-neckers.

One of his favourite pastimes is polo. He is a 4-handicap player (the equivalent of a 8 handicap in golf), and would be even better if he were a little more ruthless. His Australian friend and coach, the immensely likeable Sinclair Hill, once told me: 'He has more natural ability than his father, but if he wants to reach the top he has got to develop more of a killer streak'.

This, of course, is difficult for the Prince. If he were too rough there would be complaints from those watching. They wouldn't like to see him pulling horses around, and it is not in his nature to do so. I have seen him cry when a horse, on which he was playing, died during a game at Cowdray Park

Polo is the sport that makes easily the biggest dent in his considerable income. It costs the Prince around £15,000 to £20,000 a year, and he begrudges little of this, despite his well-known reluctance to part with money readily.

One of the less attractive sides of Prince Charles is the mean streak that runs through him when it comes to handing out cash. Be it buying the weekly groceries for Highgrove or having a slap-up meal in a restaurant, there is always a slight problem at settling-up time. It is hard to fathom out why this should be. It could be that he has rarely ever handled money and just doesn't know what things cost these days. But stories are rife about how he went into a rage when discovering the amount of a bill presented to him for payment. Despite being as rich as Croesus, he tends to query many items, strangely believing that he may be being 'done'.

Until a couple of years ago he had an 'understanding' with his detectives that at the end of a meal in a restaurant – at which the Prince was the host – a tip of 12 per cent should be left to the staff for all their troubles. The detectives, who sit at separate tables (and with their backs to the wall so they can always watch the door) traditionally pay for the meal and subsequently get paid back by Prince Charles. Nothing was ever officially agreed, but a 10 per cent tip was considered too little and 15 per cent too much. Hence the figure of 12 per cent was arrived at and was never queried by HRH.

That is, it wasn't until one day a particularly bad meal, with not very good service, was served up to an increasingly grumpy Prince Charles. Much later that night the Prince asked the accompanying detective – on this occasion Chief Inspector Paul Officer – whether he had left a tip.

'Of course', replied Paul.

Prince Charles flipped. 'How dare you be so free with my money', he shouted.

The matter did not end there. Some time later Inspector Officer received a letter, handwritten by an obviously still furious Prince, saying in future he, the Prince, would indicate the size of the tip with a series of elaborate hand signals. If the service was good (and the food as well) a certain signal would be relayed across the restaurant. If neither was satisfactory, another signal would be given and the size of the tip should be reduced. On occasions it was to be nothing at all. But whatever happened, the amount should never be more than 15 per cent!

The Prince's main income comes from properties and assets of the Duchy of Cornwall and he does not receive anything from the Civil List, money granted to various members of the Royal Family to allow them to carry out their official duties. Instead, he is entitled to the entire profits of the Duchy, which are considerable – around £600,000 last year. A male heir to the throne is automatically Duke of Cornwall, and the tradition of the sovereign's eldest son receiving this income dates back to the fourteenth century when, in 1337, Edward III instituted the arrangement for the benefit of his son, the Black Prince.

Prince Charles has not, in fact, been taking all this money until now, choosing to give half of the annual profit to the Treasury instead of income tax. But he has always retained the right to cease this gesture, and now that he has found a wife he will almost certainly hang on to every penny.

Apart from occasional hand-outs from the Queen, the Duchy is the Prince's only regular source of income. But the Queen generously keeps an eye on the finances of all close members of her family to see they are never really short. If she judges that any member of her 'flock' really does need assistance to maintain royal standards in a way that they cannot afford themselves, she will discreetly pass across the 'necessary'. Prince Charles and Princess Anne (with the purchase of Gatcomb Park, together with a number of acres as a wedding present) benefit similarly.

As Duke of Cornwall, a title he inherited on the death of his grandfather, King George VI, in 1952, the Prince is one of the richest young men in the world.

Over many years, the Duchy property was allowed to slip into a state of near decay, but after Queen Victoria's consort, Prince Albert, stepped in to completely reorganize it for his son, the future Edward VII, the Duchy of Cornwall became revitalized into a highly profitable organization. It is, in effect, a company of which the Prince is the chairman.

The Duchy owns 131,000 acres of often prime land and sites in nine different counties. As the title of the 'company' suggests, much of this land is situated in Cornwall and the West Country. But forty-four acres are in Kennington, London, where Prince Charles is landlord to 850 tenants.

Some are quite ordinary people, while others are old family retainers, like Miss Helen Lightbody, the Prince's former nanny. Others who have lived in Duchy property include the runaway MP, John Stonehouse, and the former prime minister, James Callaghan.

The jewel in the Prince's London property crown is the Oval cricket ground, leased to the Surrey County Cricket Club. But the Duchy owns other interesting sites. For example, the Prince is the owner of Dartmoor prison, which is in fact leased to the Government rent free. He also own a number of ancient castles, including those at Tintagel, Launceston, Liskeard, Trematon, Restormel and Exeter. In addition, he is proprietor of the oyster beds on the River Helford (on lease to MacFisheries) and the Duchy Home Farm at Stoke Climsland in East Cornwall, where he breeds prize-winning Devon Red Ruby Cattle.

Under ancient statute in connection with the title, he also has several strange rights. He is entitled to all whales and porpoises washed up on Cornish beaches. Similarly, all cargoes of ships washed up on the coast are his. And if any Cornishman dies without leaving a will and without any next-of-kin (about a dozen do so a year) the Prince inherits all their worldly goods. Peculiarly, he is entitled to extract fifty puffiins a year as dues from the Isles of Scilly. In fact he has never bothered to do so. But one perk he does enjoy each spring is the leg of lamb sent to him by the people of Fordingham in Dorset, who roast a sheep for him each St. George's Day.

The latest property acquired by the Duchy of Cornwall is the Prince's new Gloucestershire home, Highgrove, which will be where the Prince and Diana will spend much of their early married life. The 'company' bought the place in the summer of 1980. Although the cost was extremely reasonable at £800,000 the Duchy has had to spend nearly a quarter of a million pounds more on doing the place up to make it suitable for the Prince and his bride. Accounts vary as to precisely what has been done, but there have been extensive renovations to the structure, while one independent security expert claimed that the cost of bringing the residence up to a sufficient standard of safety was likely to be £60,000 in the first year alone.

But, whatever the cost, the idea of living in Gloucestershire (close to Princess Anne) was always more appealing than living at Chevening, the house which Prince Charles inherited from the late Earl of Stanhope. This magnificent Kent country mansion near Sevenoaks was left to the Prince because of Lord Stanhope's dream that 'one day the Prince would bring his wife to Chevening and their children would grow up there'.

In 1969, two years after Lord Stanhope's death, the Prince and the Queen looked the house over in the autumn. They both found it 'gloomy and depressing'. They were also upset that it was in such a state of disrepair. The offer was turned down.

But, a few years later, after around a million pounds had been spent on the property, Prince Charles changed his mind and decided to would like to live in Chevening after all. It never happened. He spent the odd night there, and even launched the Queen's Silver Jubilee Appeal from the house, but he showed no inclination to move in.

The residents grew fed up and disappointed that he did nothing with the place, not even shooting over the 2,500 acres. Then, early in 1980, it was announced that the Prince would never take up residence at Chevening. Two or three months later it was stated that he had bought Highgrove.

This house, bought from Maurice Macmillan, son of the former Conservative prime minister, is much smaller than Chevening, having only nine bedrooms and six bathrooms. But it is much cosier, and Diana has already said how much she is looking forward to 'doing up the place'.

Prince Charles, on the engagement day, said that he was relying on his fiancee to get everything organized so that the accommodation would soon become habitable. He obviously helped Lady Diana's task by ordering that the final wallpaper in each of the rooms should not be pasted up until she had made her own choice. That side of his life should be arranged by his wife-to-be, decided the Prince.

Highgrove, is not, as a matter of fact, their only available home. On the Duchy Estate in the Isles of Scilly he has a bungalow called Tamarisk, after the local feathery-leaved seaside shrub. But, pretty as it is, it is rarely used, and in the last five years I have only heard of the Prince sleeping there once.

It is, however, used by other members of the Royal Family for summer holidays with young children. The bungalow is close to the holiday home of another former prime minister, Sir Harold Wilson.

Unbeknown to most people, the Duchy also owns Sandringham, the Queen's Norfolk residence where each New Year is celebrated by the Royal Family, as well as the adjacent Park House where Lady Diana grew up.

And if Prince Charles should become Governor-General of Australia and want to buy property there – as a retreat from the stuffy formality of living at Government House in Canberra – the money would be supplied by the Duchy.

The 'company', which employs nearly a hundred people, has regular meetings which are chaired by Prince Charles. Naturally he likes to make sure that the operation is being run at its most efficient. He needs a hefty salary. He has to run a large office and pay the wages of a private secretary, an assistant private secretary, an office manager, several secretaries (quaintly known as lady clerks) and two valets.

Then, apart from polo, the Prince now owns a racehorse which is in training with his friend Nick Gaselee in Lambourn, Berkshire, while he also keeps several hunters for his days of sport with the Belvoir, the Quorn and his local pack of foxhounds, the Beaufort in Gloucestershire, where he regularly hunts with his sister Princess Anne.

'He has too big a bottom and short stumpy legs . . .'

Maintaining his blue Aston Martin is also expensive, while other cars he has to pay for are his Range-Rover and a Ford Granada Estate. A further major drain on his resources is the expense of dressing himself suitably for many different occasions. His wardrobe, dressing room and uniform room would not disgrace a medium-size opera house.

Two valets, Stephen Barry and Keith Stronach (formerly the valet to the late Earl of Mountbatten), are responsible for looking after all these clothes and for seeing that the Prince is always immaculately turned-out. They do a good job, even though the Prince has in his time been accused by the *Tailor & Cutter* magazine of being deliberately shabby and looking like an 'out-of-work parson'.

One of the biggest problems for the Prince is that, in the course of one day, he might have to wear five different outfits. He does not have a very good figure, with far too small a chest (38 inches), too big a bottom and short stumpy legs. Making suits for him is therefore a minor nightmare.

Two tailors have the problem: Hawes & Curtis of Dover Street, and more recently, John & Pegg of Clifford Street, who have started making suits for the Prince after previously being responsible for his uniforms.

Prince Charles, naturally enough, does not go to his tailors. His tailors, master craftsmen or not, come to him. A valet usually pops in once or twice a year to ask them for samples, and then the Prince chooses. These days grey seems to be his favourite colour.

The secrets of the fitting room are usually sacrosanct, but the story along Savile Row is that the Prince 'droops a bit on the right but has no awkward bumps or lumps anywhere'. His shoulders are sloping, which makes him a more difficult person to dress smartly than someone with square ones. It is also known that the Prince does not like flared trousers under any circumstances, and that he hates wearing waistcoats. He does like a long lapel and prefers only two buttons on his jackets. He orders about three or four garments a year. He is not particularly fussy, but he does like to be comfortable. 'His only real stipulation is that nothing should be too way out', says tailor Teddy Wilson.

'Prince Charles looks at his best in military uniforms' at the ceremony of Trooping the Colour (above) and in the uniform of a colonel of the Welsh Guards (facing page).

Prince Charles looks at his best in military uniforms, and also appears relaxed in well-cut country wear. Casual dress does not become him, and although he does possess one pair of blue jeans, it is a rare occurrence for him to put them on.

His greatest concession to trendiness is a delight at wearing jokey tee-shirts. It was while he was a serving naval officer that he started to get the habit. While captain of HMS *Bronnington* he even sketched out his own design for the ship's tee-shirt. And he still occasionally wears it. Nowadays one of his favourites is the Royal Marines tee-shirt.

Prince Charles is frustrated on occasions that his position prevents him from getting 'more stuck-in' when he might wish to. But, every now and again, he manages subtly to get his point across, striking a blow for Britain and himself. One such opprtunity presented itself to

HRH in July 1980 at the height of the 'lamb war' with France. Even as the then President, Giscard d'Estaing, was instituting yet another round in the skirmish, his personal representative was being made to eat best British lamb while dining on the Royal Yacht.

I was with the Prince on the official visit to Brest, and heard the chortles going on among the royal sailors at the cheekiness of it all; and the way it came about was this. Although the French were blockading all importation of British lamb on the very day when *Britannia* arrived, there was nothing they could do about what was already on board the Royal Yacht. As the principal guest, Giscard's representative, Admiral Jean Lannuzel, sat down to dine, his eyes nearly popped out when he saw he was about to eat lamb cutlets *à la Prince of Wales.*

10

An occasion when he had to control himself and his innermost feelings came about when he visited the British Leyland plant at Longbridge in October 1980. The speech he had to make to the assembled workforce was very different from the way he really felt about the situation. Naively, he had for ages been telling friends how he dearly wanted to be allowed to tell the workers 'all about the facts of life'.

He would say: 'If only I could make them understand how important it is for them to keep working, particularly because of the threat from foreign car workers. What I would really like is a real face-to-face, heart-to-heart chat with the whole lot – including the most extreme members of the unions'.

The Prince must have realized that if he ever had made such a speech, the whole of BL would have been out on strike at once. However frustrating it may be for him – and at times he must practically burst – Prince Charles must never get involved in political arguments like this.

Since leaving the Royal Navy, however, the Prince has started seriously to acquaint himself with all aspects of British industry and to gain a serious working knowledge of the way the country functions. The programme has included visiting the Treasury, attending working parties at No. 10 Downing Street, having tours of the Stock Exchange and even the Inland Revenue headquarters at Somerset House (why on earth should he concern himself with that?).

But, when he first came out of the Navy, he devoted most of his energies to raising money for the Silver Jubilee Appeal which distributed money to help young people with various projects.

Since then he has had nothing to occupy himself fully, nothing to stretch him to use his undoubted talents. Of course he is busy a lot of the time, attending meetings that never get talked about outside Buckingham Palace. Of course he makes frequent, often exhausting, visits abroad, as he did earlier this year to New Zealand, Australia, Tasmania, Venezuela and the United States, where he talked to President Reagan in the White House. Of course he is the International President of the United World Colleges, a group of private schools spread worldwide whose aim it is to bring together students from different countries so that they can train and study together.

But something is missing. Something is wrong when a person with the talent of Prince Charles can go off on holiday on 20 December and not get back to the grindstone until February.

The Prince always had two major problems: no wife and no real job.

Now he only has one.

The Prince leaving 10 Downing Street after making a short tour to learn something of how the Prime Minister's department works. His future subjects await enlightenment.

Cowboys and Indians, disco raver, man from the outback – the Prince adopts many guises on tour.

The Romance

I had been standing on the river bank for about five minutes when I first noticed a flash of light. It was the giveaway that was to signal the start of the greatest romance story this century. A person hiding behind a tree, just a few yards from where Prince Charles was fishing in the Dee, was quite clearly watching intently everything that was going on.

I looked closer and saw the tip of a green wellington boot sticking out by the base of a pine tree.

'I can see somebody', I said to my photographer Ken Lennox.

'Sure you can', he replied. 'And do you also notice she is watching us through a hand mirror?'.

So that was what had caused the reflection of light. What a cunning lady, I thought. This one is going to give us a lot of trouble if she is indeed the new girl in the life of Prince Charles. You had to be a real professional to behave like this one. It was clear she had no intention of being found or photographed in the company of the world's most eligible bachelor.

But I, Kenny Lennox and Arthur Edwards, a fellow reporter from the *Sun* newspaper, had completely different ideas. We wanted a picture of this girl, as well as to know who she was, and why she was hiding like this, and we wanted it immediately. The first problem therefore was to get the picture.

This was where my years of training at flushing out girl-friends of Prince Charles came into play. I went up-river to Arthur, told him that the girl was definitely behind the tree as we had suspected and suggested he train his 500 mm Nikon lens on the left-hand side of the trunk while I walked down-stream with Ken. Now I was confident that if the girl dashed away on either side we were bound to get a picture of some description, and with luck, a look at the person's face. I was wrong.

As I walked with Ken the figure behind the tree sat tight, obviously still hoping she hadn't been spotted. When she realized that she had, she stood up immediately and walked directly up a one in two hill without once turning her head. Since she had a head scarf carefully arranged around the side of her face and a flat cap on, we didn't get a clue as to who she might be.

'Often the two of us had looked long and silently at each other down the barrels of our respective binoculars.'

Charles and Harvey walking by the banks of the Dee.

She had foxed us completely and brilliantly and was clearly going to be a worthy opponent.

In the meantime, Prince Charles had been playing a very passive role. Until the previous few seconds he had continued to fish in the River Dee as if he were all alone. His concentration was not all that it might have been, and at times he was using his rod to beat salmon to death rather than to fly fish for them. But he too did not want this girl spotted by us. Least of all did he want her photographed. Too often over the previous months and years his relationships with girls had been spoiled by too much interference and attention from the press. This time he wanted to give love a real chance of flourishing without hindrance from cameramen and reporters such as myself.

So, during all this fun and games with the then 'mystery' girl, the Prince had fished on as nonchalantly as he could under the circumstances. Only when we finally flushed out the girl from her hiding place did he angrily get out of the water and start to follow her up the river bank. But, before he joined her at his waiting Range-Rover, hidden among the trees, he turned to view us through his binoculars. He wanted to know who it was who was disturbing his peace.

One of the greatest pieces of equipment that I have used in all my years of Charlie chasing and watching has been my binoculars. I have three pairs in all, one of which is always around my neck. Relatively recently the Prince had taken to carrying binoculars almost as often as I do. Often in similar circumstances the two of us had looked long and silently at each other down the barrels of our respective binoculars. And this time was no different.

The Prince stood on the bank, looked long and hard, and made a note of who was there before turning away. Seconds later he had joined the mystery girl at his car and had driven even further into the trees, his wheels spinning noisily.

We stood and reflected on what had happened and what the significance might be of this cloak-and-dagger behaviour. For this was not the only occasion we had stumbled on these two together that day. Half an hour before I had, with the aid of my binoculars, spotted the girl sitting on the river bank, watching the Prince fishing almost within the shadow of Balmoral Castle, some six miles from where we now stood.

Only a confusion of tactics between rival photographers had prevented us from getting a fully recognizable front view of the girl at that stage. The Prince and the girl had then made good their escape in the fiasco which followed, and the less said about it the better. This was the only occasion between then and the engagement announcement – still five and a half weeks away – that any photographer stood a sporting chance of getting such a picture. All Ken had been able to do was fire off three rapid frames and hope for the best.

As can be imagined, a most terrible row broke out between the newsmen. But as the curses continued to fly we were halted in our tracks when just across the river and near where the Prince had been the Queen came riding by on horseback.

In the meantime finding Prince Charles and his lady-in-hiding again hadn't been as difficult as might be imagined. One of the Royal Family's biggest faults is their predictability. They tend to do the same thing, at the same time, in the same place, over and over, year in, year out. The Scotland Yard detectives assigned to look after the Queen and her family shudder each time they think about the implications. They know only too well how this obviousness makes protecting them an absolute nightmare. But the Queen won't listen.

'We will do things when we want to do them', she says. 'We will not change our way of life'.

Prince Charles is no different from the rest. So, once he left his fishing spot near Balmoral I was pretty certain I knew where he would head for. Earlier in the year I had caught the Prince with his former girl friend, Anna Wallace, at the same salmon pool.

On that occasion we had to spend several hours finding the Prince and Anna again, but the experience paid off handsomely on the second occasion. I drove straight to the pool and there they were.

But despite all this cleverness on my part I still didn't know the name of the girl. That was supplied by Arthur Edwards later in the afternoon while we were all at the Braemar Games, one of the Royal Family's favourite events during their holidays in Scotland. By a mutual 'contact', Arthur was told that the girl who had hidden on the river bank was Lady Diana Spencer.

I was amazed, although just a month or so before I had found Diana watching the Prince play a game of polo at Midhurst in Sussex, at the beautiful home of Lord Cowdray, one of the richest men in Britain. What did her presence mean? I asked myself first. And then, asked the same question, Arthur, like me, wasn't sure. But one thing we did discover in a hurry was that the Queen was absolutely furious with us for 'disturbing the Prince of Wales while he was quietly fishing on the Balmoral estate'.

Naturally enough she had spotted the Prince being driven out of the river on the first occasion near the castle and she wanted a full list of those responsible. The police were asked to make enquiries and to report back to her. I subsequently learned that when the names of the culprits were being given to the Queen later that day she interrupted to say '. . . And Whitaker, Whitaker was there too, wasn't he?'

Anyway, returning to Diana and the significance of her being with the Prince that weekend, I had seen Diana in the Queen's house party on one previous occasion (in January 1978, at the Queen's Norfolk residence, Sandringham). Then, I had presumed that Diana was there as a companion for Prince Andrew rather than for Prince Charles. After all, she was much more Randy Andy's age group, and, in any event, Charles's girl friend at the time was Diana's elder sister, Lady Sarah! So it was rather a puzzle to work things out. From one of my informers I learned that there was 'nothing in their friendship', but that Diana had spent the last day or two following HRH around like a love-sick kitten.

'The Prince likes her', I was told. 'But she's just a baby, so for goodness sake don't get carried away with what you write'.

In the light of what subsequently happened, I could wish I had gone out on a limb and taken a 'flyer', as ridiculously over-emphasized stories based on guesswork are known in the newspaper industry. But, despite what Buckingham Palace officials and members of the Royal Family may think, I do try to get things right. So I took a sensible view and wrote a story recording that Lady Diana Spencer, the younger sister of the Prince's former girl friend, Sarah, was the girl helping to bring a smile back to Prince Charles's lips after the heartbreak of his broken romance with Anna Wallace which had ended two and half months before.

At the same time, Ken Lennox drove through the night to get original pictures, rather than wired ones which lose so much quality, to my newspaper's head office in Manchester. The story of the two being together was considered sufficiently important to warrant this sort of effort, so it was disappointing that in the event it all appeared on page 3 of the paper rather than on the front.

On Sunday afternoon I found out the plane on which Lady Diana was due to travel back to London from Aberdeen airport, and booked my own passage on it.

At the airport, Diana duly arrived with two of the Prince's best friends: Nick Soames and Andrew Parker-Bowles, both of whom had helped to make up the weekend guest party. There was no sign of Camilla Parker-Bowles, the wife of Andrew and one of the Prince's favourite married women friends, but I was much more interested in Lady Diana.

'Have a nice weekend, did you?' I asked her. For the very first time I took note of the lowering of her head that subsequently became her trademark. And, of course, the deep blush that was to become known throughout the world, though it wasn't quite so pronounced then. She just smiled back and said, 'Yes, thank you very much'.

We went through the security check together and I noted how little jewellery she had in her jewel box, which, it was insisted, she should open up. Just a gold chain and a string of pearls. Back at Heathrow, she was well guarded by Nick Soames and Andrew Parker-Bowles and I had no chance of following her further. That night I thought over all that had happened and decided to make more inquiries about Lady Diana the following day. Bells were ringing, but small ones.

On the Monday morning I called the London home of Peter Shand Kydd (Diana's step-father) in Pimlico to ask to speak to Diana. I did not say I worked for the *Daily Star* and hoped that whoever I spoke to might assume I was a friend. A youngish voice answered and explained that Diana did not actually live there.

'Where could I get her?' I asked innocently.

Clearly, however, having read that morning's paper, including the story of Diana being with the Prince in Scotland, the person on the other end of the line (whom I subsequently was told was Diana's brother, Lord Althorp), guessed that I was a reporter. He replied: 'I will tell you where she will be tonight. She is going to see her boy friend in Wimbledon tonight. You will find her at the home of __________', and he gave me a name.

Great, I thought, fantastic, I'll get an interview with 'the other man' in her life. My mind was racing. I got the address of the person and a telephone number where Diana would be. The phone back down on its cradle, I shot across to the picture desk to get a photographer standing by and impatiently waited for the time when I was told Diana would be at the address in fashionable Viewfield Road.

Diana runs the gauntlet of press photographers outside Coleherne Court. As always, she reacts with charm and good humour to the inevitable questions.

Thus I went a-hunting with news photographer of the year Frank Barrett. At the house we found that there were four flats to be investigated. I knocked on one door and was told that the boy I wanted almost certainly lived in the basement, so we rang the bell. After a pause the door opened and a man appeared. Was Jeremy Breem (which is what I will call him) in? 'Who are you?' I was asked.

After explaining we were from the *Daily Star* the man said he was sorry, he couldn't help us, and closed the door. All very strange. An hour later, and after trying all sorts of other doors and even addresses, we were back at the first one we had started off with. I tackled some students living at the top of the house as to whether any of them were called Jeremy Breem (or even whether they knew Diana Spencer), and was told that the person I wanted certainly lived in the basement.

Just as Frank and I were preparing to go and knock on the obviously correct door for a second time, the man whom I had previously spoken to and a slightly pimply, incredibly nervous boy appeared on the driveway.

The boy blinked and said cautiously: 'I am Jeremy Breem. Why does the *Daily Star* want me?'.

I burst out laughing. He looked petrified. I said: 'Is Diana Spencer with you? I gather she is your girl friend'.

He went ashen. 'That's not true,' he stammered. 'I've read the papers this morning and although I do know Diana please don't call me her boy friend'.

There was no way he wanted to cuckold the Prince of Wales.

'Well, what's going on?' I asked, feeling sorry for the chap.

'I know', he said suddenly. 'It must be her brother Charles having a game. I'm at Eton with him. The swine . . . I'll kill him'.

It was at this stage I got the break I needed.

'Where does Diana live?' I asked.

Jeremy thought for a moment and said, 'I'm not absolutely certain, but I'm sure the name of Coleherne is in the address'.

Having once had a girl friend who lived next door to Coleherne Court, I guessed that this must be the place I wanted. I thanked the still trembling Jeremy and, with Frank, shot off to the Earls Court area of West London.

There were no signs of any names on the door bells of the elegant block of flats so it was a question of persuading the porter to tell us where Lady Diana lived. That was no problem. Courteously I was shown the book containing the names of all the tenants, and there was Lady Diana's in Flat 60. Simple. Now we could investigate Lady D a little more closely.

Frank and I agreed not to make a full frontal approach by knocking on the door. We thought the best thing was to watch her for a day or two to learn her pattern. We agreed to meet outside her address the next morning. Early.

Just after 6.30, we were both in position. The agreement was no pictures if there was any chance of her spotting us. And no words. Not yet.

At 7.20, Lady Diana, tall, slim and very very pretty, emerged from the front door. Frank and I followed from a safe distance. She went shopping for milk and bread in an Indian-run delicatessen, and then went across the road to a newspaper stand to get the papers.

Frank, his fingers itching, resisted taking a snap. It was too dangerous. We didn't know enough about the lady to break our cover.

'The lowering of her head which subsequently became her trade mark...'

D

And anyway, there was no hurry. The *Daily Star* was the only newspaper in Fleet Street to have her address.

All that day we watched and waited. Twice we only followed as she drove off in a blue Volkswagen. The first occasion she went to the local shops, but the second time was much more interesting. She drove straight in at the front gate of Kensington Palace. She was obviously totally used to driving into this royal residence off Kensington Gore and clearly had done so many times before.

Diana was becoming steadily more interesting. (As I subsequently learned, one of her sisters, Lady Jane, who is married to Robert Fellowes, assistant private secretary to the Queen, lives on the edge of Kensington Palace, and this was who Diana was visiting).

Frank and I kept watch the whole of the rest of that day and were back in position the following morning. But this time Diana did not do the early-morning milk and newspaper run. Instead, a flatmate emerged and we cursed our luck. In fact, we had already been spotted, and the girls inside No. 60, Coleherne Court were getting very nervous as to who Frank and I might be. Various curtains in the flat kept moving back, and a head would disappear quickly when we looked up.

We held a hurried conference and agreed we ought to reveal ourselves as we were not in the business of trying to scare people half to death. So, when one of the flat-mates appeared (it was Carolyn Pride), I walked up to her, said where I was from and apologized if any of them had been worried.

Said Carolyn: 'I must admit we were. But thank you for coming forward now, and, yes, Diana will be out in a minute'.

Sure enough, five minutes later Lady Diana arrived at the front door.

'Could we take pictures', we asked.

'Why?' she riposted.

'Because you are very pretty and you are the girl who is bringing happiness back to Prince Charles', I replied. 'Well, all right', she said. 'But don't be long, I have to go shopping.'

I decided to ask the question that so many people were beginning to ponder over.

'Is it true that you are in love with Prince Charles?' I asked.

Then came that famous blush that I had seen once before. And the nicest smile that I have ever encountered. But she wouldn't confirm anything. She nodded her head, shook her hair and drove away.

I wrote a story for the *Star* that day, calling her the woman with 'a secret'. Although I didn't believe for a second that Prince Charles was in love with her, I was beginning to accept that Lady Diana could easily be in love with him. She seemed so perfect. And, even more, few people in society seemed to know her. It was all to her advantage.

With the publication of a second exclusive story in the *Daily Star*, Fleet Street started to feel uneasy. Phones grew red hot as reporters tried to find out more about Shy Di, as she was beginning to be called. But number one on everybody's agenda was to find out where she lived.

Frank and I had the address on our own for only one more day before word started to get out. From then on – 12 September – until the day of the engagement – 24 February 1981 – Coleherne Court was rarely left unguarded by somebody from Fleet Street.

But the next major development came when it was discovered that Lady Diana was a teacher at the Young England Kindergarten in St. George's Square, Pimlico. And, on 17 September, two dramatic and significantly important things happened to Diana. Nigel Dempster, the incredibly influential *Daily Mail* diarist, devoted the whole of his page to her. And she posed, unwittingly, for the most sensational pictures to be taken of a woman who will one day be Queen of England.

Nigel's column on the morning when he gave her his seal of approval took the whole story from one of great interest to one of monumental proportions. Like it or not, it was from this date that everybody – possibly even Prince Charles himself – started to take the romance seriously. Dempster recorded that the two 'happily married women who influence Prince Charles most on personal matters, Lady Tryon and Camilla Parker-Bowles, have both given the heir to the throne their approval over his new choice of a girl friend'. He went on: 'Now the way is clear for Charles to plight his troth to Lady Diana Spencer who, friends tell me, has secretly worshipped him for most of her life'.

All of this was true. I knew it, and most of Diana's family were aware of her adoration for the Prince. But now it was out in the open.

That same morning Frank Barrett and I arrived at Lady Diana's kindergarten school to try to get pictures of the girl of the moment. We had heard that she just might be prepared to pose for a few minutes to try to persuade photographers to leave her alone while she was teaching young children. It will never be fully known whether Buckingham Palace officials had any hand in this decision or whether it was the headmistress of the school, Kate Seth Smith, who urged that it should happen. But happen it did, and with devastating consequences.

The Young England Kindergarten (complete with Young Englander) where Lady Diana worked.

'I knew your legs were good. But I didn't realize they were that spectacular. And did you really have to show them to everybody?' (Right) the famous 'see-through skirt' incident.

Diana appeared shyly from the front door of the school building – which is, in fact, a Boy Scout hut – with two sweet and tiny children on either side of her. We were asked not to name the tots because the parents had not been consulted, and this was agreed. We were also asked not to press Diana with any questions. This was not agreed.

In the end, Diana didn't say much of interest anyway. She mumbled something about not wishing to say anything about Prince Charles, and added: 'You know I cannot'. I asked her if she had been instructed to say nothing by Buckingham Palace, and she replied: 'No, that is not true. It is my decision'.

But the sensational aspect of this session was what the photographs showed. At first, Diana sat demurely on the ground with a child on each side, and just looked a little bit sad. Then, when photographers wanted a change of scenery, they asked her to go and stand over by some bushes so the sun could come shining through her hair.

Only at this stage was it realised by the half-dozen or so cameramen present that the setting made Diana's Liberty print skirt almost completely transparent because of the low angle of the sun. What happened was a fluke. There was no devious plot to put Diana in a somewhat embarrassing position. Nobody knew that day that she wouldn't be wearing a petticoat. But, as soon as the photographers saw how much they could see of her legs, Diana was destined to end up all over the world.

I suppose Lady Diana might have wondered a little bit more shrewdly why the photographers would keep asking her to go back to the same spot by the bushes, to 'walk this way one more time'. But she didn't. It's not part of her nature. Co-operation and being pleasant to everybody, including the gentlemen from Fleet Street, was the name of her game – certainly at this stage of the courtship.

News got out quickly that Lady Di had posed for pictures. Before long scores of other photographers were turning up at the school to ask if they could have pictures too. Sweet Diana accommodated everybody. By lunchtime she had given three photo sessions for a total of some twenty cameramen, but the only snaps that will be remembered are the ones which show her legs.

Regrettably she will go down in history as 'the girl who forgot to put on her petticoat', as she has since admitted. It was not until lunchtime that day that she realized what she had done when a representative of the Press Association – an agency which supplies pictures and stories to many, many newspapers in Fleet Street and throughout Britain – arrived at the Young England Kindergarten to ask if they too could have a photo session. A copy of the *Evening Standard* was waved at Lady Diana, revealing everything from that early-morning photocall.

Diana nearly died. She certainly cried when she realized that the pretty skirt she had always loved so much was almost completely see-through.

'Is there nothing I can do to get this picture out of the paper?' she appealed.

'No', she was told kindly but firmly. 'In fact, wait until tomorrow morning and you will find yourself in a whole lot more newspapers'.

Indeed, there wasn't a single popular paper the following Thursday morning that didn't have a huge picture on page 1.

The episode made the nation catch its breath. It also taught Diana a sound lesson. It taught her to be careful. She wasn't made to feel cheated or tricked. Her friends explained that what had happened was 'just one of those things'. But never again was Diana to agree to anything without 'thinking it through' first.

Prince Charles, I understand, was thoroughly amused by the whole episode.

'I knew your legs were good', he is said to have told Diana. 'But I didn't realize they were that spectacular'. Teasingly he added: 'And did you really have to show them to everybody?'

After the excitement of the morning, it was time to think about the whole business in terms of what it all meant.

Girl friends of Prince Charles had never posed for pictures before. They normally ran away. Real girl friends of Prince were discreet about their relationship. So why was Diana saying things like, 'You know I cannot talk about my feelings for him'?

There is no doubt in my mind that Lady Diana was getting over her 'besotted' feelings and was, by now, 'in love' with HRH. For his part I believe he was 'very fond of her' and found her freshness and naivety enchanting. But he was certainly not in love with her at this time. His feelings were still very much for his previous girl friend, the fiery, tempestuous Anna Wallace who had so publicly jilted him during the summer.

However, after this explosion of publicity the two got together and decided that a low-key, even more discreet series of meetings would be the way to play things from now on. They were brilliantly successful in their scheming. Their next public sighting did not take place for a month.

The occasion they chose to attend together (if not side by side) was a race meeting at the West Midlands racecourse of Ludlow. Prince Charles was there to ride his own racehorse, Allibar. Lady Diana, in a warm overcoat, was there to cheer him on. And she did so both noisily and with a reasonable degree of success. As the horse jumped the final fence and started to surge into second place, Diana, red in the face, jumped up and down and squealed with excitement.

I was standing at her shoulder and noticed she could barely watch as the man she loved slowly cut back the lead that the eventual winner had over him. It was a very revealing moment. Although I had never doubted her affection, here was positive proof that she was crazily in love. With Judy Gaselee (the wife of Prince Charles's trainer Nick Gaselee) and Camilla Parker-Bowles at her side, she ran to welcome the Prince into the unsaddling enclosure.

Only two photographers on the track, the *Daily Star*'s award-winning photographer Stan Meagher and Arthur Edwards, knew Diana was at Ludlow at this stage of the afternoon. But, despite her excitement, Diana was still clever enough to make sure that no cameraman got the Prince and herself together. A pact had been made by the two by now that they would never willingly be pictured in the same frame. And, to the end, they succeeded.

Charles, Diana and Princess Margaret enjoy a day at the races before the watching punters.

Highgrove House.

After the race Diana told me that she had had a small bet on the Prince – for a place only. Which may have been prudent, but was hardly terribly trustful of the Prince's ability! Since, as time went by, the Prince started to develop his nasty habit of falling off horses during races (which happened at Sandown Park and, a few days later, at Cheltenham) her judgement can't really be faulted.

An hour after the Prince's race, the rest of Fleet Street woke up to the fact that Diana was at the track and pandemonium reigned. Fights broke out among photographers to try to get a picture and Diana was forced to spend rather more time than usual hiding in a lavatory. As soon as the meeting was over, Prince Charles shot off in one car and Diana, moments later, in another. The police blocked the road after they had gone to give them time to join up in the Prince's blue estate car. And then they were away. But to where?

It didn't take long to find out. They went straight to the beautiful Wiltshire home of Andrew and Camilla Parker-Bowles, where they spent the next two days. Not alone and not always together. But it was a very significant weekend in their relationship.

It was during these forty-eight hours that the Prince first realized he might be falling in love with Diana 'just a little'. Until this moment Prince Charles had regarded Diana as a 'very amusing and jolly – and attractive - person.' Now he started to view her differently. They were reported as having a candle-lit dinner together, and she was spotted running down the drive of the Parker-Bowles's house to greet HRH when he returned from a day's hunting with the Beaufort. She retreated rapidly when she saw press people advancing at almost the same moment.

The following day, a Sunday, Prince Charles decided the time had come when their relationship should be stepped up. He took Diana to look round Highgrove, the Gloucestershire mansion he had bought in July from Maurice Macmillan. It was a house he had bought 'just in case' he found the right girl to marry. He wasn't at all sure that Diana would be this person, but neither was he at all sure that she wasn't.

They spent two or three hours looking over the place and they both liked what they saw. Could this be home for them one day? Diana was confident. Prince Charles wasn't. Neither was Lady Diana's mother, Frances Shand Kydd, wife of the landowner, Peter Shand Kydd. She said, during this very same weekend, 'I have three daughters and the Queen has three unmarried sons. They have all been invited to stay at Balmoral and Sandringham. Diana has recently been invited back for the fourth time – so she obviously hasn't blotted her copybook'. Yet after it was learned that the Prince had taken Diana on a guided tour of Highgrove, people began to read even more into everything.

My peers at the *Daily Star* had been anxious for a few days that I should start preparing 'a background' on Lady Diana. Following this weekend I was happy to begin. So, for the next few days, I started to ring anybody and everybody who had ever had anything to do with Lady Diana from the cradle to the present day. The idea was that I would forget about a feature I was preparing on Prince Charles to coincide with his thirty-second birthday (on 14 November) and concentrate instead on a one-day (possibly two-day) feature on Lady Di.

The continuing problem with writing anything about the Royal Family is that the entire system, orchestrated by palace officials in league with friends of the Royals, is arranged so that nobody is very happy saying anything. The Buckingham Palace press office denies almost everything as a matter of course – or makes such remarks as 'I just wouldn't know the answer to that' or 'You don't really expect me to answer that, do you?' – while friends don't talk. Otherwise, they wouldn't be friends for long.

Obviously I have over the years cultivated 'contacts' and people who know members of the Royal Family, who trust me not to let them down and who, in return, help me.

I have two friends, both members of the Royal Family, who help me often. I have another contact who is in a senior position at Buckingham Palace; another who holds a position of trust at Windsor Castle. I know people who work at Balmoral Castle in Scotland and others who 'help out' at Sandringham. They can never be named for obvious reasons.

It was, at all events, to people like these that I turned in preparing my background piece. I also spoke to Lady Diana's former headmistresses, her girl friends and her relatives. By the time I had finished researching the article I was convinced that this nineteen-year-old girl, who had already begun to captivate the heart of the British public, was going to become the Princess of Wales – given time and understanding.

Diana's uncle, Lord Fermoy, came up with the most incredible quotes while I was speaking to him about his niece. He talked about Diana being a virgin. This was very, very important to her chances of becoming Prince Charles's wife. Two or three years earlier I had written that, however unfair it might be in this permissive age, any bride for the Prince must be seen to be a virgin. Nothing has made me change my mind. And here was her uncle agreeing.

In a sensational interview, which has since been quoted many times, he said 'Diana, I can assure you, has never had a lover'. Proudly talking of his niece's wholesome reputation, he also said: 'Purity seems to be at a premium when it comes to discussing a possible bride for Prince Charles at the moment. And after one or two of his most recent girl friends I am not surprised. That [a lover] is what one means nowadays when talking about whether such and such a person has ever had a boy friend. And no, Diana, to my knowledge, has never been involved in this way with anybody. This is good'.

Continuing to sing Diana's praises, Lord Fermoy (whose mother, Ruth, Lady Fermoy, is a Lady-in-Waiting to the Queen Mother and one of her best friends) went on: 'I believe Diana to be quite an exceptional girl. She is extremely well liked in the Royal Family and especially by the Queen. She is very pretty and she adores children. What people love about her is that she has such a charming manner. She gets on well with people and everybody just has nice thoughts about her. She really doesn't have any blemishes. Sadly, I don't see as much of her as I would like'.

Lord Fermoy was not alone in his sentiments. My colleague, Pat Codd, spoke to Barbara Cartland on the same day about what she thought about Diana. Until now, this formidable lady with her huge hats and her passion for writing romantic love stories (there have been more than 300 published to date) had refused all interviews. But on this particular day she loosened up after listening to Pat's persuasive tongue. She said that she believed Lady Diana Spencer had the vital quality to make her the next Queen – her purity.

'The ideal for a perfect marriage', she said, 'must be a pure wife. In his heart every man – whether he is the man in the street or Prince Charles – wants to marry a woman who doesn't sleep around. Certain people must have someone young and pure'.

Of Prince Charles, Miss Cartland said: 'Whatever he does he has got to have a pure young girl'.

Of Lady Diana she said: 'I don't think she has had a boy friend. That is marvellous in this day and age because you know what girls are like now – they have sexual affairs almost before they leave the cradle. It is frightening'.

All pretty, far-seeing, excellent stuff. But Miss Cartland then spoilt it a little by adding: 'I wouldn't want my daughter to marry the Prince. Quite frankly, I think royalty should marry royalty.'

In fact, Miss Cartland wasn't utterly right about Diana never having had a boy friend. It seems that the one man for whom she did have some feelings before being courted by the Prince was a Guards Officer called Rory Scott.

Rory, aged twenty-one, a lieutenant in the Scots Guards, gained universal recognition for his carrying of the regimental colours at the Trooping the Colour ceremony in 1979. A television documentary about the Trooping featured him prominently: how he got fit, how he trained and how he performed on the great day in front of the Queen.

So how keen was Diana on Rory? 'She liked him very much', I am told. But there was never any question of hanky-panky, even though 'she used to take his shirts back to her Kensington flat to wash and iron them'.

She even used to admit that she enjoyed doing so.

But the fact remains that Rory, who was serving in Kenya before the wedding, is the only man ever 'linked' in any way with Diana. Discreet fellow that he is, he has always refused publicly to discuss anything about her.

The quote about virginity became a headline. The *Daily Star* called Lady Diana 'The Rose without a thorn', and we had an exclusive story that was light years ahead of anybody else in Fleet Street.

The idea of running a one- or two-part series was dropped. Instead we ran the story for four days, leading right up to the Prince's birthday on the Friday.

Nigel Dempster's 'approval' story in September may have boosted everything at the start – my series in the *Daily Star* took the romance into orbit. It even made people believe that there might be an engagement announcement on Prince Charles's birthday, four days later. I never thought so, but clearly there was to be no turning back for the Prince from now on. The great British public would have lynched him if their beloved Diana had been hurt in any way. She had grown more popular than he by now.

And I am pretty sure he knew it.

As the Prince's birthday approached, Fleet Street fever escalated. Lady Diana's Coleherne Court flat was never left unattended, and neither was the kindergarten school at which she was teaching. Rumblings started about press harassment and other such unpleasantness. For anybody who was covering the story fully at the time, this was nonsense.

Diana, in the main, liked the attention she was getting. She enjoyed the company of several of us, and she realized that if she were to ever become the Princess of Wales she would have to put up with an enormous amount of publicity and press attention. The stakes she was playing for – and make no mistake, she knew exactly what she was doing at all times – were high. And she never wanted to duck out of the action.

One of the first remarks she made while being interviewed on her engagement day is significant. Prince Charles was speaking about the day he asked her to marry him. He said: 'I asked Diana just before she went to Australia – I wanted to give her a chance to think about it – to think if it was all going to be too awful . . .'

Before the Prince even finished speaking, Diana chipped in and said 'Oh, I never had any doubts about it.' As somebody who spent days and days with Diana, I witnessed at first hand her determination at this point of the relationship.

'Shy Di' was always a silly tabloid cliche that made headline writing easy. Diana isn't particularly shy. She just used to blush a lot. She is a girl with a lot of guts and she is naturally charming and very sweet, even if she loathes being so described. But, having said all this, she was still vulnerable.

Most girls while being courted can totally rely on their boy friend to help and support them – not only mentally but physically. During the whole of Lady Diana's courtship she was never able publicly to turn to Prince Charles for assistance. He just wasn't around when she wanted a helping hand. He couldn't be.

In fact things were far, far worse than this. It really was a case of Prince Charles whistling and of Lady Diana running to him. The Prince was so determined to keep their romance away from the public that she had to use every subterfuge in her repertoire to get to him without people such as myself finding out. It meant that she had to carry her own, often heavy suitcases into the car without assistance, then she had to drive herself hundreds of miles – often through the middle of the night – to be with HRH.

At all times, in other words, she had to do what he wanted. I often felt very sorry for her. No normal boy friend would ever get away with treating his chosen girl in such a cavalier manner.

JA
83

It was a tough way to treat any girl, let alone one who was going to become the next Queen of England should the courtship end in marriage. And there were times, when, almost out of sheer frustration, Diana came close to tears. (She once admitted to me towards the end: 'I have cried three times during the last few months. But I promise not to do so again').

It was in the light of all this that I decided to write a letter to Lady Diana. I didn't consult anybody except my news editor, Brian Steel, but it was written on behalf of Fleet Street. Roughly, it said: 'This is to say that we, all of us in Fleet Street, love you very much. If ever we do anything that ever upsets you – which, of course, will happen – we are very sorry'. It ended by saying, 'Keep your chin up and keep going.' At the same time I sent flowers.

Two days later Lady Diana approached me outside her flat while I was waiting for her to return one evening.

With photographers snapping around her she turned to them and said: 'Please, leave me alone for a second. I want to speak to Mr Whitaker in private'.

We talked for about ten minutes about many fairly inconsequential things, but it was the start of a bond that I hope will always exist. I was certainly very moved, and if ever I had any reservations about Lady Diana they were removed for ever that late afternoon.

But the most important point about this chat was that she understood we were doing a job, that she realized we liked her, and that, apart from the odd dirty trick by foreign *paparazzi* photographers, she liked us.

On the morning of Prince Charles's birthday, Lady Diana went missing from her flat. Although it was well staked out, she slipped away unnoticed very early and, as I subsequently discovered, went to collect a brand-new Mini Metro car which had been delivered to her sister's home in Kensington Palace.

Only very rarely did Lady Di show annoyance at the intrusions of photographers, as happened (left) at Nick Gaselee's stables. Her Mini Metro soon began to act as a magnet in drawing them to her Coleherne Court flat (right) and leading them into hair-raising car chases.

In the meantime I had gone to Wood Farm, one of the Queen's residences on the Sandringham estate, to report on the birthday boy. On the way there I called in on an old friend of mine – Lady Sarah Spencer. Not only is she Diana's big sister, but she is also an old girl friend of the Prince. I had got to know her well in 1978 while reporting her romance with HRH.

As I knocked on the door of her home near Grantham where she now lives with her former Guards Officer husband, Neil McCorquodale, she opened it and said 'Hello, James, I wondered when you would be around'.

Sarah is good fun, very pretty like Diana, and forthright in what she has to say. On this occasion she chided me by teasing: 'What are you going to do when they don't announce their engagement on his birthday?'

'Don't accuse me of saying that will happen,' I said. 'But what is going to happen in the future?'

Lady Sarah paused. She wouldn't commit herself that far ahead. That was always one of the nicest habits of the Spencer girls. They never lied. It was always Diana's great boast to me. 'I have never lied to you yet', she would say. Only right at the very end she did. But then she had to.

After leaving Sarah I went on to Sandringham and spent Prince Charles's birthday watching him hunt. That evening was the birthday party at Wood Farm. Would Diana be there or would she not?

Buckingham Palace press office was saying nothing. They said they didn't know what was happening because the event was a private one. All I can say is that it is hard to retain much privacy when there are 300 or 400 journalists standing outside your front door. And yet we were all totally conned that evening.

If I had had more faith in one freelance girl photographer, Jayne Fincher, I might not have been, but I felt I needed more evidence. Jayne, the twenty-one-year-old daughter of the world-famous photojournalist, Terry Fincher, promised me that evening that she had seen Diana at the wheel of a Mini Metro (at that stage we only knew vague rumours about her having bought such a car).

Jayne insisted that she had seen Diana and the car at the side of Sandringham House. Was she sure? 'Pretty certain', she said. So with that information and a further confirmation from one of my 'contacts' I wrote a story saying that Diana was celebrating the birthday with the Prince, the Queen and Prince Philip at a small dinner party at Wood Farm.

Minutes before edition time another contact – who had never been wrong before – said unequivocably: 'Lady Diana is not at Sandringham. And she won't be all weekend. She isn't expected'. I was aghast. I rang my paper immediately and just managed to get the story killed.

In disgust at apparently having wasted my time – and also quite appalled at so many journalists waiting outside a place where I was led to believe nothing of interest was going on inside – I drove 130 miles back home. I needed to return to sanity.

Very early the next morning I received another telephone call, telling me that my informant had been misled and that Diana had been at the birthday party after all and that she was going to be at Sandringham all weekend. I got into my car and drove the 130 miles back to Norfolk.

All Saturday and most of Sunday the three of us who knew that Diana was in the vicinity searched for her. After Sunday church we got a break. A red Mini Metro was found locked up in a garage on the Sandringham estate and I was told that the car was Diana's.

Soon afterwards, while keeping watch on it, I saw it move. It was taken to a back road that leads up to the rear of Wood Farm. I was tipped off that Diana would be coming out of the farm, down that private secret lane. I just had to be patient. If I could see, with my own eyes, Diana coming off the royal estate it would be a great story, one of real significance. It would also mean that senior police officers had been lying. On the night of the birthday party an inspector had stood with the journalists outside Wood Farm and declared: 'I will swear on a stack of bibles that she (Lady Diana) is not inside'.

For the event I linked up with my old friend Arthur Edwards of the *Sun*. We decided that, to pull this one off, the first team should be brought into play. Although we are on rival papers, there are times when co-operation is bigger than anything.

I worked out that the way to handle the situation was for me to drive and for Arthur to get in the back seat so he could work a camera from either side. We then floated around near the secret rear entrance praying that our information was right. It was.

Soon after 3.30 we were rewarded. A police Range-Rover poked its nose out on to the road and, joy of joy, fifty yards behind came a red Mini Metro. My binoculars told me that Diana was at the wheel. The police car saw her off the estate and then left her, believing she was now on her own and that she would have an unmolested run back to London – with the whole of Fleet Street round the other side of Wood Farm.

I drove ahead to a nearby roundabout, circled it slowly, waiting for Diana to arrive at the same roundabout, and then drew up alongside her. What a picture her face made. She couldn't believe it, but . . . she laughed and laughed and laughed. She also blushed a bit.

There then came one of the most amazing car chases that a member (or close friend) of the Royal Family has ever been involved in. At speeds of sometimes 80 mph (and remember, Diana's car was brand-new and therefore being run-in!) I drove alongside the future Queen of England while Arthur was leaning out of the back window.

We went along the straight in this position – with my car about three feet in front so Arthur could get an almost head-on picture – and we went round several roundabouts too. Happily, Lady Diana never lost her nerve for a second, never tried to move the steering wheel too sharply, and just concentrated on driving. My reward came the following day when I had a page-one story in both the *Daily Star* and the *Sun* while Arthur had pictures in the same two papers. It was a great team effort.

But while this chase was going on, the reporters and photographers left behind were not entirely wasting their time. After Diana had slipped away, several journalists 'caught' Prince Charles down by the kennels at Sandringham where he had gone to take his gun-dog Harvey for a walk.

One said: 'We rather hoped that Friday would be a rather special day for you'.

The Prince replied: 'So did everyone else'. Rather crossly, he then added: 'I don't know what you are all doing here. Why don't you go home to your wives?'

The Prince still wasn't giving any hints at all.

In the meantime, trouble was brewing for Diana back at th' mill. Prince Charles was preparing to leave for India on an official tour and an ugly story about Diana 'secretly joining' Prince Charles on the Royal Train while the Prince was on official business in the West Country was gaining credence. The *Sunday Mirror* had printed it and a number of people believed it to be true.

The 'facts' of the story as told by the *Sunday Mirror* were that on two nights – 5 and 6 November – Lady Diana had joined Prince Charles on the Royal Train while it was in a siding for these nights. She was alleged to have stayed on board for several hours. The implication was obvious.

Both Prince Charles and the Queen were furious. The Queen's press secretary, Mr Michael Shea, was instructed to write a letter to the editor of the *Sunday Mirror*. It was a letter almost without precedent. And it provided even further proof that the Queen wanted nothing to upset the relationship between her son and Lady Diana. It really was a case of a mother hen protecting her young.

As a rule, fictitious scurrilous stories are ignored by the Royal Family. But on 17 November, a Monday, Mr Bob Edwards, the *Sunday Mirror* editor, received a letter emphatically marked 'NOT FOR PUBLICATION'. Mr Shea was, he said, writing to protest in the strongest possible terms about this story and its innuendoes, which were 'totally false' and a 'total fabrication'. It went on to request a printed apology in a prominent position at the earliest opportunity.

Mr Edwards, clearly convinced that his original story was true, stuck to his guns. The following Sunday, 23 November, he printed not only his own letter replying to Michael Shea, but also a later exchange of letters between himself and the Palace when he invited Mr Shea to send him an official denial which he would print in full.

The basis of his case was that the *Sunday Mirror* did not publish reports wantonly or recklessly, that he continued to believe that the original report had been true in all essential matters and that he was satisfied it in no way reflected badly on Prince Charles or Lady Diana.

Mr Shea then promptly reiterated that there was 'no truth whatsoever in your story, and it was denied on the express instructions of those most closely involved at Buckingham Palace', whose veracity would be impugned should the allegations be repeated.

From a journalistic point of view, I can only admire the way Mr Edwards made the best of those two letters. I am sorry to say, however, that no apology was ever forthcoming, but what could Mr Edwards do if he still believed he was right and accurate?

Although I was utterly convinced myself that Lady Diana didn't go near the train that night, the story clearly needed further investigation. In the week following publication of the letters I decided to do a little digging. Ken Lennox flew down from Scotland to help.

We talked to locals in the area who knew where the train had spent the night. We talked to railway officials who knew the movements of the train. But, most important of all, I got hold of the official log which detailed every second that the train had been in the West Country. And, not to give anybody away, I spoke to a person who had had the train under surveillance on one of the nights Lady Diana was supposed to have been on board.

Not one person I spoke to in those two days believed there was any truth whatsoever in the *Sunday Mirror* story. Moreover, I also knew that the story was being denied by the Queen herself, not to mention the

Prince of Wales. If the *Sunday Mirror* wasn't one hundred per cent certain either way, surely they could not believe that the Sovereign and the heir to the throne were lying. If it was proved that they were, it could feasibly have been the beginning of the end of the monarchy. The British people have a right to expect total honesty from their Head of State.

Despite all this, it seemed to me that the one way to kill the lie stone dead would be to approach Diana herself and say, 'All right, if you weren't on that train, what *were* you doing?'

By now I was pretty much on speaking terms with Lady Diana and she showed no hesitation when I stopped her on her way into her flat after she returned from shopping. Would she like to clear the whole business up once and for all? 'Yes' she said, she 'would welcome the chance'.

The following day we led the *Daily Star*'s front page with a story marked 'Exclusive':

> Lady Diana Spencer yesterday appealed to the *Daily Star* to 'print the truth' about her alleged nights of love with Prince Charles on the Royal Train.
>
> 'I am not a liar', she said. 'I have never been on that train. I have never even been near it'.
>
> And she added 'If you explain what really happened I hope it will end all the speculation and innuendoes that have put me in such a bad light'.
>
> Then Lady Diana revealed her REAL timetable for November 5, one of the nights when, according to the *Sunday Mirror*, she was smuggled aboard the Royal Train in a siding at Staverton, Wilts.
>
> In an exclusive interview at her South Kensington home 19-year-old Lady Diana said:
>
> 'I stayed in all that evening with my three flatmates, Virginia, Carolyn and Anne. Please believe me. I am telling you the absolute truth.
>
> 'I had some supper and watched television before going to bed early. I had been at Princess Margaret's party at the Ritz the night before and I was feeling very frail and hungover.
>
> [She has since denied using the word hungover to me. But I quoted her as saying 'hungover' in the full knowledge that Diana doesn't drink at all and I will always maintain that she did say hungover.]
>
> 'I didn't feel like going anywhere and I never moved out of the flat. My flatmates will testify to this'.
>
> Pretty Virginia Pitman confirmed Diana's story. She said: 'I popped out for an hour to go to a bonfire party, but Diana didn't want to come.
>
> 'She was here when I left about 7 o'clock and she was still here when I got back. She went to bed early and was here in the morning. She definitely never went out'.
>
> Lady Diana went on to deny reports that her blue Renault car was seen near the Royal Train on November 5 and 6 [which was stated in the original *Sunday Mirror* story].
>
> She said: 'I wasn't driving the Renault that week. It is my mother's car which I borrowed after my Volkswagen crashed.
>
> 'It wasn't even in my possession on the two nights I am said to

have been down in Wiltshire. My mother had it. I was driven around all week in a white Fiat belonging to a friend'.

She added: 'Most people do believe that I never met Prince Charles on that train. I have had a lot of letters supporting me which are very comforting.

'But the allegations have not put me in a very good light. It has all been rather upsetting, but more than that, I am very disappointed that the people who printed the story in the first place won't believe me'.

Going back to the night of Princess Margaret's party on November 4, Lady Diana said: 'Although I believe Prince Charles left about midnight, I stayed on until 2.15 in the morning when I was given a lift home to my flat where I arrived about 2.30.

'I went straight to bed, feeling great but very tired. I certainly did not go out anywhere.

'The following night, November 5, I was too tired to go anywhere and stayed in with my flatmates'

The Queen is said to be furious about the *Sunday Mirror*'s allegations and Buckingham Palace has dismissed the story as 'absolute rubbish'.

And now I can reveal that the Royal Train wasn't even at Staverton on the night on November 6 (as stated in the *Sunday Mirror*).

The official log book shows that it had been in the siding on November 5 while Prince Charles dined with three officials of the Duchy of Cornwall.

But it left in the early evening of the sixth with the Prince on board and did not return.

So now, to believe the *Sunday Mirror* story still, you would have to think that Lady Diana was also lying. It stretches the imagination beyond belief. Certainly the *Daily Star* story took the steam out of the situation, and today there are few people who'd believe that Lady Diana ever was on that train. But as I said, there has never been an apology. Instead, a new campaign was begun (I don't know by whom) which suggested that perhaps it wasn't Diana who was with the Prince on those two nights, but some other lady. I don't believe it.

Before the second story appeared, however, the *Daily Star* had already scooped the world by printing an interview with Lady Diana which, however brief, proved to everyone that her feelings for the Prince were very, very strong. It had happened a few days before on the very Sunday when the Prince flew from London for an official tour of India and Nepal.

I had been keeping a round-the-clock watch on Diana in the firm belief that she must surely see Prince Charles before he flew off for such a long absence. Absolutely nothing of significance had happened as the Sunday drew nearer. Diana simply spent her time going to the kindergarten school, visiting friends (where the Prince was nowhere in sight) and shopping.

At 12.15, just before Sunday lunchtime, Lady Diana came out of her flat in a hurry, looking just smart enough to be heading for Windsor Castle and lunch. She jumped into her, by now, famous Mini Metro.

Apart from myself and the *Daily Star* photographer, Tim Cornall (on his enormously powerful 1000 cc motor-bike), she was spotted by representatives of the *Daily Mail* and the *Sun*.

As she pulled away in her car, so we followed. It became like one of the chases in a Keystone Kops farce. And I nearly lost Diana before the game had really commenced.

Diana had brilliantly worked out that, if she drove in a certain direction from her flat, which meant going round side-streets in a sort of square, she could 'hit' the lights in Old Brompton Road just as they were changing from yellow to red. This meant that, time after time, she would 'dump' pursuers at this spot who were not prepared to cross lights that were red on an often busy and dangerous road.

That morning the order ran: one *Sun* photographer on a motor-bike, Tim Cornall on his motor-bike, myself in a car, a *Daily Mail* reporter in his car, a *Sun* reporter in her car, and another *Sun* photographer in his car.

As Diana came to the lights, they turned from orange to red just as she knew they would. The *Sun* photographer went with Diana, but Tim, because the roads were wet, started to stop. How I didn't hit him in the rear I will never know.

But of one thing I was certain. After waiting a total of some eighteen hours a day for half the previous week, I wasn't going to lose Diana now – particularly as I was confident she could well be going to see Prince Charles. So I pulled my Cortina around Tim, put on my headlights, hooted my horn and pressed the accelerator to the floor.

I have never been able to apologise to the driver of the Rover who was already, quite rightfully, almost half-way across the lights when I flashed across his bow. But, thank goodness, he had quick reactions and stopped. I was through. I looked up and saw Diana roaring with laughter. She then turned round and shook her finger at me, and also mouthed the words, 'Naughty, naughty, you shouldn't do that'.

'Naughty, naughty, you shouldn't do that.' Lady Di at Broadlands.

Diana then headed straight towards Windsor, but although we drove past the very gates of the castle, she never went in. Instead, we ended up at Eton College where her brother, Lord Althorp (the one who had set me up with the bogus 'boy-friend') was waiting.

By this time, Tim Cornall and all the rest had caught us up on the M4, having guessed, when they had lost Diana at the Old Brompton Road lights, that this was the direction she would take.

Lord Althorp – Charles to his friends – jumped into Diana's car and gave her a kiss on the cheek. We then followed them to a nearby restaurant – the Hind's Head at Bray.

Well, we had a story, but she was with quite the wrong Charles, however happy Diana clearly was to see her brother. For all the trouble we had caused Diana during the chase, apart from following her to the restaurant, we pursuers decided to buy the couple a bottle of champagne.

When it was taken to their table we had a charming message back saying that they thanked us very much for the thought but they were both drinking orange and, in any case, Diana never drank alcohol. So, instead, we put the money towards the biggest box of chocolates that could be found.

One of the staff volunteered to go and buy the box of chocolates since none of us dared to leave the restaurant. Sadly, Lady Diana and her brother did depart before the chocolates were brought back, and in the end she never got anything. They do say it's the thought that counts.

On leaving, there then started another crazy chase and we ended up back at Eton College where Lady Diana dropped off her brother. It had all been good fun, but it wasn't really getting me very far with the romance story I was hoping to write about Di and the Prince of Wales.

So, as Diana was seeing her brother into his house, I went across to speak to her before the others could follow. I had time for one quick question: 'Diana, why aren't you with Prince Charles this weekend?'

Her reply was startling and gave me the first indication that marriage really could be on the cards. She said in almost a whisper but with enormous intensity: 'I wanted to be with him this weekend before he left for India. But we decided it was better not to get together because of all the fuss and bother it would have caused'.

She meant 'fuss and bother from the press', of course, but it was the sort of answer I had been looking for. She was a totally honest, decent, uncomplicated girl who had been seeing the Prince regularly for the previous two and a half months to my certain knowledge, and perhaps for longer, for all I knew. And I was getting a totally honest, decent, uncomplicated answer. It was something she kept saying: 'I have never lied to you, Mr Whitaker'.

There was another thing. From the very beginning she never called me James. It had always been 'Mr Whitaker'. All Prince Charles's previous girl friends – and I was friendly with them all – had always called me James. But Diana never would, even when I asked her to. That had always made me suspect that she could be the one.

Another pointer in her favour, which I always thought significant, was when she traded in her German Volkswagen for a very British Mini Metro. How could anyone serious about marrying HRH possibly drive a German car?

Before I could ask Diana anything else, rival reporters closed in on us and I backed away.

'Come on, tell us what she said', they asked. 'Come on, let's have it'.

'You must be joking', I replied.

And then, before anything else could be said, we were all off again, following Diana and her little Mini with the number plate MPB 909W.

Only two newsmen besides myself stayed with Diana as she headed back for London. And we all got stopped as she swept through the 'Private Road' sign into Kensington Palace. Without a second thought I dashed round the other side into Millionaire's Row, where all the embassies are, to try and catch her. I needed desperately to speak to her more. It was turning into easily the most revelatory day I had ever witnessed with any of HRH's girl friends.

After twenty minutes of waiting and searching I decided to walk up into Kensington Gardens to see if she could be there. With my binoculars I carefully scanned the entire park beyond the range of the naked eye. And then, as in those old naval war films with the captain scanning the high seas for 'U' boats, I came across Diana. She was sitting on a bench, with her head back and on one side. And she was clearly lost to the world.

It was a touching scene, and one that should never have been intruded upon – least of all by a journalist. But it was imperative I should speak to her and should do so without rivals being present. I checked that the other two were still round by the entrance to Kensington Palace and started to walk across the park and towards the bench.

After I had gone some 200 yards I turned round and saw Howard Foster of the *Daily Mail* watching me. He clearly hadn't seen Diana, but he was obviously intrigued about what I was up to. He started to follow.

I increased my speed as I needed to get to Diana before Howard could arrive to overhear what was being said. I really didn't want to intrude on Diana's thoughts. If I had been on my own, I wouldn't have acted so. I would have waited; for a long time if necessary.

But Howard was getting closer. In fact he was almost running by now. As I came within hearing range of Diana I called out, 'Diana, believe me, I *am* sorry to disturb you but I must ask you something'.

Until that moment she hadn't a clue anyone was close to her. She shook herself out of her faraway mood and smiled.

'Yes, what do you want to ask me, Mr Whitaker?' she said.

I turned round to see where Howard was and realised I had hardly a moment to play with. As at Eton, I had time for one question. I said, quite clearly, so it wouldn't have to be repeated: 'Are you going to marry Prince Charles?' There was a second left to add: 'Do end all the speculation that's building up'.

She thought for a moment before replying very deliberately: 'I really don't know'. It wasn't a 'no comment', it wasn't even what she said that was important. It was the way she said it with a heavy sigh. I knew at that moment that she and the Prince had obviously discussed marriage. Whatever was said later about the proposal being made just before Diana went on holiday to Australia in early February 1981, I will always be sure in my own mind that, by 23 November 1980, they had at least talked of marrying.

After the reply to my first question, I had to risk a second before Howard Foster reached us. I said: 'Is it true that the Prince has already asked you to become his wife?'

There was a further pause before Diana, now with tears in her eyes, replied: 'I can't say anything. I just can't say anything'. Again, it wasn't what she was saying – which on the face of it was nothing at all. But I could understand it all from the way she looked so tense and worried.

At this stage Howard arrived and we started to talk about the weather. I couldn't give any indication of what I had just learned. We all chatted happily for some time, and I asked Diana crazy things like how to pronounce the family's courtesy title Althorp.

'Is it Althrup, Altrup or Althorp?' I asked.

Said Diana: 'Some of our family pronounce it Altrup. I personally say Althorp. It's all a matter of choice.'

Her father, Earl Spencer, also says Althorp, despite what the 'experts' state.

I also asked Diana how many 'O'-levels she had, believing that the information would come in useful one day. At this she went all coy.

'Well, do you have more or less than your sister Sarah?' I asked, adding, 'because she has six'.

'About the same', said Diana laughing.

'Does that mean four or five?' I replied.

She laughed louder and started to blush. 'I'm not going to answer', she said. 'I am sure you will find out soon enough, Mr Whitaker'.

Well, I still don't know, but it has been suggested that she might not have any. Diana's scholastic career was never particularly academic, but there is no doubt that, even in those far-away days, she was always very popular with her contemporaries.

At her preparatory school, Riddlesworth Hall, at Diss, in Norfolk, her former headmistress, Miss Elizabeth Ridsale, remembers her as a girl who was 'always a decent, kind and happy person at school. She was a perfectly nice little girl, always cheerful with the others, and that is how she has gone into adult life'. She was also good with animals and is remembered for her pet rabbit.

The fourteen-year-old Lady Diana.

A family photograph taken in 1969. Left to right: Richard Wake-Walker, Lady Anne Wake-Walker, Miss Elizabeth Wake-Walker, Captain Christopher Wake-Walker, the seventh Earl Spencer, Diana, Charles Spencer (now eighth Earl), Countess Spencer, the Hon. Sarah Spencer, Viscount Althorp and Jane Spencer.

At the age of thirteen Diana went on to West Heath School, near Sevenoaks, in Kent, where she is recalled as a girl with a ready smile who played hockey and lacrosse well, and swam well. Just three years later, at the tender age of sixteen, Diana left this school to go, albeit briefly, to a finishing school in Switzerland, the exclusive Institut Alpin Videmanette in Rougemont. She learned two very useful things in the few weeks she was studying here: how to speak French fluently and how to ski well.

Mrs Shand Kydd told me: ‘People are always surprised to learn that Diana was only at this school from Christmas to Easter. But that was how it was always planned. She really only went there to learn skiing and there isn't too much snow in the summer!’

Her French teacher, Madame Barbara Fuls, remembers having a telling conversation with Lady Diana at this time. She once said to Madame Fuls: ‘I will only ever marry for love – not for money or position’.

Even in those days, Diana loved children.

‘She knew she wanted to work with children’, said Madame Fuls, ‘and then she wanted to get married and have a family of her own. But she said that love was the most important thing in a marriage’.

While at finishing school, Diana also took domestic science lessons, and learned dress-making and cooking.

The owner of the school, Madame Heidi Yersin, was ‘surprised’ when Diana did not return to the school the next term to take some exams.

'Most of our pupils stay for a year and sit our exams. Lady Diana just didn't come back and we were not told why'.

Friends say that Diana never would have been an academic, but that she can match even the Queen in terms of downright practicality and common-sense. Anyway, who wants a boffin as Princess of Wales?

That late afternoon we went on to talk about her skiing, about her flatmates, how much she loves children, how one shouldn't jump red lights while following her trail. In fact, we talked about almost everything except Prince Charles. That is until the very end of our conversation, when she said: 'One thing I don't want is a postcard from India saying "Wish you were here".'

She really does have a great sense of humour, which she will certainly need over the years to come. In fact, it is her greatest of her many assets. The final question before we left was whether Diana would be going to Heathrow Airport to say good-bye to the Prince.

'No', she said. 'I am going home and will stay in all night'.

As I left Diana I felt happier than I ever had since becoming a journalist. With the main page one story in the *Daily Star* the following day – carrying another 'exclusive' tag – I knew that I had cracked the big one. I couldn't say for sure when the day would be. But I could say it was only a question of time.

Lady Diana, however, was learning how to handle the press the hard way. A private conversation which she thought she was having with a lady neighbour – who also happened to be a freelance journalist – appeared as an 'exclusive interview' in the *Daily Mail* on the same day as mine, though it did not contain any of my essential material.

It did quote her as saying about all the press attention: 'The whole thing's got out of control. It's not so much boring for me but boring for the public seeing my face in the paper every day. I'm not so much bored as miserable. Everywhere I go there's someone there.'

Her next experience came a few days later when she found a few polite answers she had given in an interview with a Press Association reporter 'souped up' into an 'exclusive' which put words into her mouth about her wish to be married soon, among other things, and repeated her denial about the Royal Train story.

No sooner had I read the Press Association release than I was on the telephone to Lady Diana and found her close to tears. 'I didn't say any of this,' she told me, 'I am amazed. All I talked to the reporter about was the story that I was meant to have been on a train with Prince Charles. I just repeated and confirmed the story that was in the *Daily Star*'.

The outcome of all these 'exclusives' was that Diana's mother, Frances Shand Kydd, entered the fray on behalf of her daughter with a letter to *The Times*. In doing this Mrs Shand Kydd was only thinking of her daughter. But it was written without reference to Lady Diana and without her knowledge.

'Sir', wrote Mrs Shand Kydd, 'May I through your columns put truth and reality into the newspaper reports concerning my daughter, Diana Spencer?' There have been many articles labelled 'exclusive quotes', she complained, when the plain truth was that her daughter had never spoken the attributed words. Did the editors of Fleet Street, she asked, 'consider it fair to harass my daughter daily from dawn to dusk?' Was this fair treatment for anyone, regardless of circumstances, and did it not represent an abuse of press freedom?

I must admit that this letter raised my own ire in turn. Mrs Shand

Kydd had not even begun to look into the circumstances of the so-called 'harassment'. What she thought was going on was pure guesswork, and so she was doing precisely what she accused the pressmen of doing.

Lady Diana, in a telephone conversation, told me she did not agree with what her mother had written, though she realized it had only been sent off 'to help'. 'There are times when press people upset me', she confirmed. 'But this is very rare and I like to think I get on very well with most you. The only thing that really annoys me is when my children (at the kindergarten) get frightened by things like flash guns.'

From my own observation, Lady Diana knew the names of the 'regulars' and would call out a cheery 'Good morning' to each and every one. She would almost invariably add the person's name.

For the first time in my life, I was poised to write a letter to *The Times* myself, to put the record straight from the journalist's side. I even went so far as to draft one.

In twenty years as a journalist on numerous newspapers, I can truthfully say I have never known a more popular subject with the public. Of course this interest means newspapermen waiting at her home to see what she is doing, where she was going, what she has to say. We had no other means of getting direct or accurate information. The Buckingham Palace press office gave nothing away. We could hardly ask Prince Charles himself.

On the other hand, I could vouch for Lady Diana always having answered my questions freely and frankly with no objections, and for not replying to a question if she did not wish to. It seemed to me that she was aware of our basic affection for her.

My letter was never sent as my editor felt it was better to 'leave the matter alone'. He did, however, add a comment with which I thoroughly agreed: 'I understand your concern that *Times*-type people criticize us for just doing our job, but we don't need to defend ourselves in public when we are right. You and I have nothing to be ashamed of. Our readers are the judges not the readers of *The Times*'.

But after everything was said and done (or maybe undone) some good did come out of all this furore. Speaking to Diana as a friend and not a journalist, I called on her later that week to have a chat. I told her plainly: 'Diana, if you go on talking to the press as much as you have done lately you can only damage any chance you might have of marrying HRH. It is not liked by the Royal Family and I urge you to stop'.

I went on: 'Don't ever lose your charm to us, your sweetness, in fact everything that makes you such a lovely person. But do stop talking. There will be times when I will ask you a question to which I need an answer desperately. I am telling you now, *don't answer me*. I know I am cutting my own throat, but I believe that marrying Prince Charles is very much more important than me writing another exclusive'.

Quite separately from this conversation, I then went round to the flat to speak to Diana's flatmates, Carolyn Pride, Virginia Pitman and Anne Bolton. I spoke specifically to Virginia.

'You have got to help Diana more', I said. 'You have got to give her more protection. This whole business is getting out of hand. She'll end up losing HRH and that would be disastrous'.

Virginia replied: 'We do help her, we do everything we can for her and, honestly, we are sure she is all right. But it is very difficult at times'.

I pressed again: 'Well, try even harder. And whatever else, for God's sake, stop her talking'.

Despite all my good and well-intentioned advice, I still had to carry on covering the story. And a really big weekend was coming up with the return of Prince Charles from India and Nepal.

To help me I asked Kenny Lennox to come down from Scotland once again. He arrived on Thursday, 11 December, and his arrival began nine of the most exhausting and time-consuming days of my life.

Ken and myself averaged nearly eighteen hours a day, either with Lady Diana or within a few yards of her. Sometimes I got some relief, as on one occasion when I had to go and write a feature in the office. Or when I went off to watch my sons play rugger for their school or club. But Ken just kept going.

Our sole aim was to stay alongside Diana so that, should she join up with the Prince, we would be there too. Some of the adventures Lady Diana, Carolyn Pride, Ken and myself had during those few days will remain with me for ever.

There were moments when things became fraught, but it was during this time that I got to know Diana as a friend and to become convinced that if Prince Charles didn't marry her he would have missed out on a real gem. Diana would laugh when I said to her: 'If he doesn't marry you he will be a fool'. She was most likely laughing at me. She knew perfectly well then that it was all on. Meanwhile, in India, the Prince was being equally coy and non-commital – certainly to all press inquiries.

He told Harry Arnold of the *Sun*: 'If only I could live with a girl before marrying her. But I can't. It's all right for chaps like you. You can afford to make a mistake, but I've got to get it right first time. And if I get it wrong, you will be the first to criticize me in three years' time.'

The Prince, to another reporter, said: 'You know you mustn't rush me. What you don't understand is that because a girl stays in the same house overnight, well, it isn't a case of 'here we go, hooray and whoopee'. It simply cannot be like that. In my position I have to live a rather old-fashioned life. And so do those in my circle'.

When Paul Callan of the *Daily Mirror* commented, at the same cocktail party, on how well Diana was coping under pressure, the Prince replied: 'That's kind of you to say so. I must say I think she has been magnificent'.

It was therefore surprising that after his return to Britain, it should be a whole week before the two saw each other again. During that period Diana, nearly always with Carolyn at her side, led Ken and me a merry dance as she tried to give us the slip.

On one occasion she went through the fire exit of a Knightsbridge shop to get away. Her escape included climbing over dustbins to get out! On another, she and Carolyn jumped on a bus before, after five yards, it became stuck in a traffic jam, so allowing us to catch up. A hilarious sequence followed as Diana tried to duck away from having her picture taken sitting on a number 45. It soon became clear that she had obviously not travelled on such a conveyance for years. As she was getting off – after travelling a distance of eight yards – she offered the conductor a 10p piece.

The beaming West Indian replied: 'Have this one on London Transport, Lady Di'.

By now she was a well-recognized figure as she went on her shopping sprees around Knightsbridge, Fulham, Chelsea, or Bond Street. Sitting at the wheel of her Metro she was even more noticeable. But always with love and friendship by the great British public. Without exception they would shout such comments as, 'Good for you, Di'. Or,

Charles on his Indian visit.

'How's Charlie? I hope it all works out well for you'. On one occasion I heard a man say: 'He'd better do the decent thing by you, or I will want to know the reason why'. It was becoming clearer and clearer that Prince Charles would face losing all his popularity if ever he jilted Diana. Such an action would not have been liked at all.

During these few days there were other incidents that did not involve Diana trying to get away from Ken and myself. In fact she was extremely grateful to us during many of her outings, especially in the West End. Since it was just before Christmas, there were never any meters or parking spaces free and on many occasions we would fend off traffic wardens while Diana went shopping in the big stores.

Diana would say: 'Look, I won't be gone very long but do keep an eye on the car for me. I'd hate a ticket'. The wardens, who normally have little regard for anybody parking illegally, even if they are the girl friend of the Prince of Wales, couldn't do enough to help.

'Is that Lady Diana's car?' they would say. 'Oh yes, of course it is. I recognise it now. Yes, of course it can stay there. She's a lovely girl isn't she?'

Once, when she was in the Bond Street area, Diana stopped off to go into Collingwood's, the Queen's jewellers in Conduit Street. I still don't know for sure why she was there that day, but she was jolly keen not to be photographed coming out.

When she did emerge, Ken said to her: 'How many stones are there in the ring you have just chosen?'

'Thousands', she replied laughing.

'But are they sapphires and diamonds as most girls want?' I asked.

She giggled. But that was precisely the make-up of her engagement ring when it was finally revealed on 24 February!

On the same day I asked again, for the hundredth time, why she hadn't seen HRH since his return.

'You mustn't ask', she said. 'I can't say anything.'

And I knew that this was true.

The following day, Wednesday, 17 December, was destined to be one of the most momentous for Diana in her whole relationship with Prince Charles. It was all fairly dramatic for myself as well. We had received a 'tip-off' from a contact that *The Times* had a whole page prepared for use in the following Friday's issue. The implication was that it could contain the official announcement of the engagement. Moreover, it was whispered, the person who had 'chanced across' the page being prepared had been sworn to secrecy to say nothing, not even to admit he had seen it. It looked a strong possibility that the story was about to break.

More than happy to check the rumour out, I waited from 11.00 onwards that night to put it to Diana. Earlier in the evening, she had promised me that she was just going off to see a friend – not Prince Charles – and would we let her go without us following. We had agreed.

At 11.50, while Ken and I were waiting in total darkness across the road from her flat, we saw Lady Diana turn up in her Mini Metro. Although Ken was frantic to get a picture – which would have been spread on the front page if there should be confirmation of an engagement – I felt that words were more important.

I urged Ken that we should stay out of sight until she had locked up her car and was heading for the flat. But by then it was too late. I'm not sure how, but she spotted us. She was gone.

She'd unlocked her car, jumped into it and pulled away from the kerb with shrieking tyres. Kenny and I leaped back into our car and tried to follow. By now we were utterly convinced that the story was true. Why else should she bother to shoot off like that?

Diana turned left off Old Brompton Road with us still 150 yards behind and promptly disappeared. Cursing at our luck, we toured the area for the next fifteen minutes, trying to see if she'd parked and was hiding.

I then rang the paper to say what had happened and to confirm that it looked as if the story could be true. Page One would be kept open, they said. All I had to do was stand the story up!

But where were we to go? My idea was to drive over to Kensington Palace to see if she had gone into hiding with her sister, Lady Jane, and her brother-in-law, Robert Fellowes. Ken's idea was to go back outside the flat and to wait there. I agreed we'd do this, but for no longer than ten minutes, I said. Ken's hunch was right, however. Within five minutes Diana came cruising slowly by again in her Metro.

Nearly giving myself a heart attack, I pulled out and started to follow her once more. She wasn't going to give us the slip this time.

For five more minutes we cruised around the totally deserted streets before Diana returned once more to the street outside her flat and parked. I stopped some fifty yards away and walked slowly and warily towards her, ready to dash back to our own car at a moment's notice if she should take off again.

She didn't. She got out, carrying a basket, and said sweetly: 'Good evening, Mr Whitaker. How nice to see you.'

'Why did you dash away like that?' I said. 'You'll make me suspicious.'

'Like what?' she replied. 'I've just got here. I haven't been dashing anywhere.' But there were more important things to consider. Ken and I could hardly discount the evidence of our senses. With Ken taking picture after picture – and Diana ducking out of view as only she knows how – I then asked the big question: 'Is it true that your engagement to Prince Charles is being announced on Friday?'

Diana said nothing.

I went on: 'We have information that the announcement will be in Friday's *Times*. Is this true?'

All the smiles and joking stopped. It was serious, and she knew it.

I then said: 'This is just about the most important question I have ever asked anybody in my journalistic life. Diana, I wouldn't be bothering you at this time of the night unless I was in deadly earnest. This is very, very important.'

Lady Diana then said: 'I know. I understand what you are saying and I will treat your question with respect. Obviously this is all very serious. But will you stop Mr Lennox taking pictures?'

I turned on Ken and snarled: 'For God's sake stop, Kenny. For God's sake leave her alone for a second. I must talk to her without you going on and on.'

Poor Ken. Here was perhaps one of the most important moments of his journalistic career, poised to get the picture that could go all round the world. He did stop for a moment, but every time Diana moved, the camera would come up and another picture would be shot off.

Eventually, Diana said: 'Let's go inside the block of flats where we can talk', and we went through the glass doors leaving Ken behind.

We then started to talk, sometimes standing, sometimes sitting on the stairs. We talked for a total of nearly an hour. To begin with, Diana was giving away very little. But when I said that if she would not deny there was to be a Friday engagement I was going to write a story that night, she became most concerned.

'Please, Mr Whitaker, do be careful,' she said urgently. 'There is so much I want to explain to you, but I can't. This is very, very difficult for me. I want to help you so much, but I mustn't. You must understand how hard this is for me. I want to help you . . .' Her voice trailed away.

She had so many loyalties being stretched in so many directions. When I told her that on the basis of what she had just said and her refusal to deny the possibility of engagement I was going to write the story anyway, she froze.

'Wait a moment,' she said. 'Look, please go and check your information more. This is so difficult . . . but be careful.'

We talked on quietly for another twenty minutes to half an hour. Eventually, when I said that I was not going to write the story after all she gave a big sigh and said: 'Good. People have once again got excited too soon.'

Throughout the whole of that highly emotional midnight chat, Lady Diana managed to retain her sense of humour. And although she was clearly worried she also remained marvellously calm and controlled. Once again, she was showing that, when it came to the crisis, there was nothing shy about Di.

In fact, just as I was finally leaving her and was going out through the glass doors into the street, she called me back. Laughing, she said: 'That was quite a conversation. One day you and I will have to write a book about it all.' She knew her business, how to handle each passing difficulty and how to keep everybody with whom she came into contact totally on her side. She could charm dustmen, hard-bitten journalists, children in her kindergarten and, of course, her darling Prince Charles.

But there was one other person with whom Diana had needed to make her peace. It is realized by only a handful of people to this day that, during her courting period with Prince Charles, she had to make one other person fall in love with her. Without the affection and unqualified approval of the stuffy, staid Mr Edward Adeane, her chances of marrying the Prince of Wales would have been much reduced.

The royal party at a Wiltshire game fair. Edward Adeane is second from the left.

Mr Adeane, nine years older than Prince Charles, replaced Mr David Checketts (now Sir David Checketts) as the Prince's private secretary in 1979.

He had been a friend of the Prince for some years previously, sharing HRH's love of fishing and shooting. He also comes from a long line of devoted servants to the Sovereign. His great-grandfather, Earl Stamfordham, was private secretary to Queen Victoria before becoming private secretary to the Duke of York before he was Prince of Wales and then later King George V. His father, Sir Michael Adeane (now Lord Adeane), was assistant private secretary to King George VI before becoming principal private secretary to the Queen from 1953 to 1972.

Edward Adeane himself was a page to the Queen, so is well known and respected in the Royal Family. He is also very, very powerful. He was formerly a libel barrister, numbering *Playboy*, *The Times*, the Tory party and Lady Falkender among his clients. Thus he can also be persuasive of tongue.

What he had to say about some of Prince Charles's girl friends was frightening. Anna Wallace, the one before Lady Diana, is capable of testifying to the fact. So is Sabrina Guinness, the girl friend before Anna.

As a bachelor himself, Adeane didn't like either and did much to discourage Prince Charles away from their charms. He particularly fought with Anna, who used to clash sharply with him over his not having a wife of his own.

Lady Diana was much more clever. She realized early on in her relationship with the Prince that she must get Adeane on to her side. She teased him gently about being a bachelor, calling him an old fuddy-duddy. She made him laugh at his sober, ultra-conservative approach to life. But, most of all, she convinced him that Prince Charles had never met a more serious contender to be Princess of Wales than Lady Diana Spencer.

A Buckingham Palace courtier who watched the wooing of Adeane in progress told me: 'It was incredible to watch Diana at work. She worked it all beautifully. She soon had Adeane eating out of her hand and, by the end, I think he was almost as much in love with Diana as was the Prince.'

After my midnight chat with Diana I was convinced that there was going to be no engagement for at least a month, and definitely not one during the Queen's Christmas Day message, as many believed. Two days later, Diana gave Ken and myself the slip – despite all our hard work and watching – and, as I learned later, went to Scotland and to Birkhall, the Queen Mother's home, to be joyously reunited with Prince Charles.

She ditched us professionally and completely. She did so by walking out of her flat with a suitcase and putting it in the back of her Mini Metro. A few minutes later, she re-emerged with a green husky jacket and a pair of green wellington boots which she placed alongside the case. When she came from the flat yet again she was dressed in an old scruffy coat and started to walk towards the Earls Court Road. It was presumed that she was going to get something from the shops as she had done so many times in the past.

I was called quickly from the office where I had been writing a feature on Prince Andrew and told Ken 'to get here with double speed' as it appeared that Diana was leaving for the weekend and that we should be following. I had a look in the back of the Metro, and sure

'She ditched us professionally and completely'. Diana's Mini Metro and the suitcase which fooled the author.

enough, there were the suitcase, the coat and the pair of boots. Nearly forty-eight hours later, all three items were still in the car which hadn't moved.

Ken and I had been well and truly filleted. That weekend Ken returned to Scotland, not totally defeated but pretty severely bruised. I felt the same.

The following Tuesday, 23 December, I did catch up with Diana. I went round to her flat to congratulate her on her disappearing act and to wish her a Happy Christmas. She opened the door, wearing a blue dressing gown and red pyjamas. And she didn't look too good for a change.

'How are you?' I asked breezily.

'Not too well', she replied. 'In fact I feel awful. I've got flu.'

I resisted asking her what she had been up to at the weekend and instead asked if there was anything I could do. She replied that she thought everything would get better if she stayed in bed.

'Have you called a doctor?' I asked.

'No, it's not that bad', she said.

Teasingly, I then asked Diana if she believed in homeopathy.

'Homy . . . what?' she said. 'What on earth is that?'

I replied: 'If you are going to become the daughter-in-law of the Queen you had better learn about homeopathy. That is her favourite form of medicine.'

I went on to explain that homeopathy basically involved treating diseases, aches, pains and colds with natural medicines. For example, bruises are smoothed away by rubbing arnica on them, and there are even homeopathic cures involving the use of snake venom and the extract of the plant commonly known as deadly nightshade.

Diana was intrigued. She didn't know that the Royal Family were great supporters of this strange technique, popularized in the eighteenth century by a German called Hahnemann. I said I would arrange for some homeopathic medicine to be delivered to her to try and cure her flu.

I went straight to a chemist in Duke Street, asked them what they recommended and was given a white box containing pills. Since I had a journalists' lunch to attend, I then had to find a taxi to deliver the precious package to Lady Diana.

The cabbie I stopped in Oxford Street went open-mouthed when I told him what I wanted him to do.

'Do you mean *the* Lady Di?' he said. 'The one who is meant to be going to marry Charlie?'

I nodded, explaining that I wanted him to go to her flat, No. 60 in Coleherne Court, to ring the bell and tell Diana that he had come with something from James Whitaker. I gave him a fiver and said to be sure he went at once. This he did, and so Diana took her very first homeopathic pill.

When I saw her after Christmas – which she spent at home at Althorp with her father and stepmother – I asked her how she had got on with them.

'Terrific for about twenty-four hours', she said. 'They dried me up completely and I didn't have a runny nose at all. But then, when the effect had worn off, I think my cold was worse than ever.'

With Christmas over, it was time for the Royal Family, led by the Queen, to decamp from Windsor Castle and head for Sandringham in Norfolk. Traditionally, I had done the same for the previous few years, and this season was to be no different.

In fact, with Diana likely to surface at the estate at any moment, it was essential to be in residence at the same time. Naturally, I was not alone in my thinking. The area was crawling with press for most of the time. In fact, complaints by the Queen were relayed to reporters and photographers, and once, she actually and unprecedentedly shouted, 'Why don't you go away' in a tone more suitable to a commoner than the Queen of England; and Prince Edward fired a shotgun over the head of a *Daily Mirror* photographer.

All in all, those few days were a fair shambles with hardly anybody emerging with much credit. But the all-time low came when Prince Charles sent his 'unhappy' greetings to Fleet Street editors. The message came as a bolt from the blue on 3 January.

It was a Saturday, and I was standing at the village hall in Anmer watching the royal shooting party go for their picnic lunch. I didn't really believe that Diana would be with them – it would be too much to hope for, but one never knew.

The last person to go into the green hall, which is opposite the Duke of Kent's courtesy house, Anmer Hall, was Prince Charles. He had been giving his labrador, Harvey, a run. At the last moment he hesitated and came across to a group of some dozen or so journalists who were waiting.

'I should like to take this opportunity to wish you all a very happy New Year and your editors a particularly nasty one,' he said.

He then walked away, only turning back when he heard one of their number shout after him: 'Well, I don't wish you anything nasty, Sir . . . Happy New Year.'

Prince Charles replied: 'That's very kind, thank you.'

As if this wasn't worrying enough, there was one additional problem: what on earth had happened to Lady Diana? At this stage I still didn't know about that secret weekend in Scotland before Christmas which was only revealed by the Prince and Diana on their engagement day. So as far as I was concerned, I couldn't say for sure that the two had met since the Prince's return from India. Obviously they must have done, but when and where was another question. Stories even began to appear in the national press, suggesting the romance might be 'cooling'.

On Thursday, 8 January, my reward came for many hours of seeking and digging, and many days of getting up at 5 am to begin another stint that almost certainly wouldn't end until midnight.

On that morning I left London with Steve Wood, a reporter on the *Daily Express*, and a freelance photographer called Tim Graham, who has supplied many of the photographs in this book and who is known as 'Secret Squirrel' for all the confidences he keeps so well. Our plan was to head straight for Highgrove to see if Diana might just be with the Prince there since I had discovered that HRH had gone missing from the royal party at Sandringham.

Half-way down the M4 we stopped at a service station to get a quick cup of tea and a refill of petrol. Just as we were driving away, Steve suggested: 'Would you like to check Gaselee's place first?'

Nick Gaselee is Prince Charles's racehorse trainer, and we knew that HRH quite often went there in the early morning to take his then racehorse Allibar for an exercise gallop. It seemed a good idea since it was hardly out of our way and in fact it turned out to be a masterful suggestion. We drove round the corner of the cul-de-sac in which Mr Gaselee lives at Lambourn, and there, outside his front door, was Lady Diana's red Mini Metro.

The *Daily Star* story the following day was simple and to the point. It had a headline saying: 'Charles and Di Together', placed under a smaller heading saying: 'Pictures prove the romance is not cooling.'

The whole of the front page was taken up with it and three pictures were used. One showed Diana emerging from the Gaselee house after breakfast, another showed Prince Charles coming out of the same door and a third showed Charles's Ford Granada parked alongside Diana's red Mini Metro.

In the story I was able to reveal that Prince Charles and Lady Diana had seen each other secretly at least three times since he returned from India, and that the latest meeting killed growing reports of a cooling romance.

The Prince had gone riding before breakfast, and Lady Diana watched him intently as he galloped across the Lambourn hills in the early morning light. Then the Prince had ridden back from the stables on a battered old bicycle, pausing just long enough to call out to me a cheery, 'Hello, you're up early.'

Proof positive that the romance wasn't cooling: Charles and Diana are seen together at Nick Gaselee's home.

They had breakfasted together before Lady Diana had to return to Windsor for the funeral of Princess Alice of Athlone. Lady Diana was expected to join the Prince at Sandringham before the holiday ended.

And so she did. But there was so much activity and running about when she did arrive in Norfolk that she didn't stay long. At the same time, some of the Fleet Street 'heavies' – the so-called 'quality' newspapers – continued to wage war against the popular press as it reported all the comings and goings of members of the Royal Family.

In writing an article about these problems I said how it was a 'love-hate' relationship that continuously existed between the Royal Family and the media. At times they needed us badly to relay all that they were up to and to record what a good job they are doing. At others, they tried to retreat into their palatial shells, to pull across their thick damask curtains and pretend the rest of the world didn't exist.

The sort of full-scale invasion that had taken place during the previous nine days at Sandringham was certainly not to their taste, but it was hard to know what they would have been saying privately if not a word or picture had appeared in the newspapers during that period. Very probably they would have been concerned, including the Queen.

Not so long before, in West Africa, Prince Charles had turned to me at a cocktail party and said quite earnestly: 'You know, the time we all have to worry is when you don't write words about me or want to take photographs. Then there would be no great point in us being around.'

The difficulty came in deciding when the 'Royals' were on holiday and should be left alone, whether they ever were entitled to 'have days off'. For myself, I didn't believe that they ever should be left alone. The Royal Family live in quite magnificent splendour. Their many homes (Windsor Castle, Buckingham Palace, Sandringham House and Balmoral Castle to name but a few) are not only huge but are set in many thousands of acres. Should they wish to get away from prying lenses or inquisitive reporters like myself, it was perfectly easy for them to disappear into the middle of their grouse moors or rolling acres of countryside, or behind huge brick walls.

Only for a few moments each day were we possibly near enough to upset them. On the other hand, it was regrettable that there should be clashes between *them* and *us*. If only they weren't so brilliant at what they do in public life, I said, we wouldn't be so interested in everything they get up to.

At times they could all be so incredibly naive. If the Queen had a cold, it made page one of most newspapers. If Princess Anne fell off a horse, the news made banner headlines round the world. So why should they show dismay and surprise at reporters spending so much time at Sandringham in the hope of Prince Charles's girl friend Lady Diana Spencer turning up.

There was nobody who 'covered' the Royal Family, I said, who did not love and respect them. But relations were not as good as they might be. When the Queen said: 'Can't you leave us alone?' and shotgun pellets rained down on press cars parked by the roadside, the situation was due to be reassessed.

The clashes were nothing new. For several years I had received lectures from Prince Charles, Princess Anne and their aides about granting them some peace. I had been called a perfect pest and been warned that if I did not move from a certain spot I would be arrested or, even

With breakfast on his mind, Prince Charles pedals hard towards his rendezvous with Lady Diana at Nick Gaselee's Lambourn home.

worse, be hit by stray shotgun pellets. At other times, and in between these occasions, I had spoken at some length with members of the Royal Family in situations where there had been nothing but laughs, jokes and smiles all round.

The Royal Family had always adopted Disraeli's adage, 'Never complain, never explain.' They had always been above sueing over inaccurate stories, complaining about untruths or entering into arguments concerning their private lives. The public respected them for this attitude, and most people I knew wished the Royal Family to continue in this way. But times were changing and the Royals should keep pace.

Why couldn't they be a little bit more co-operative in explaining what was or wasn't happening? Why couldn't we be told officially whether Lady Diana Spencer would be spending a weekend at Sandringham? After all, most people hoped and believed she would marry Prince Charles before long. So why should we have to ferret and cajole Royal servants to give us a piece of information that could and should have been provided by Buckingham Palace.

Temporarily separated from Lady Diana, Charles sets off for the slopes at Klosters with Patti Palmer-Tomkinson in tow.

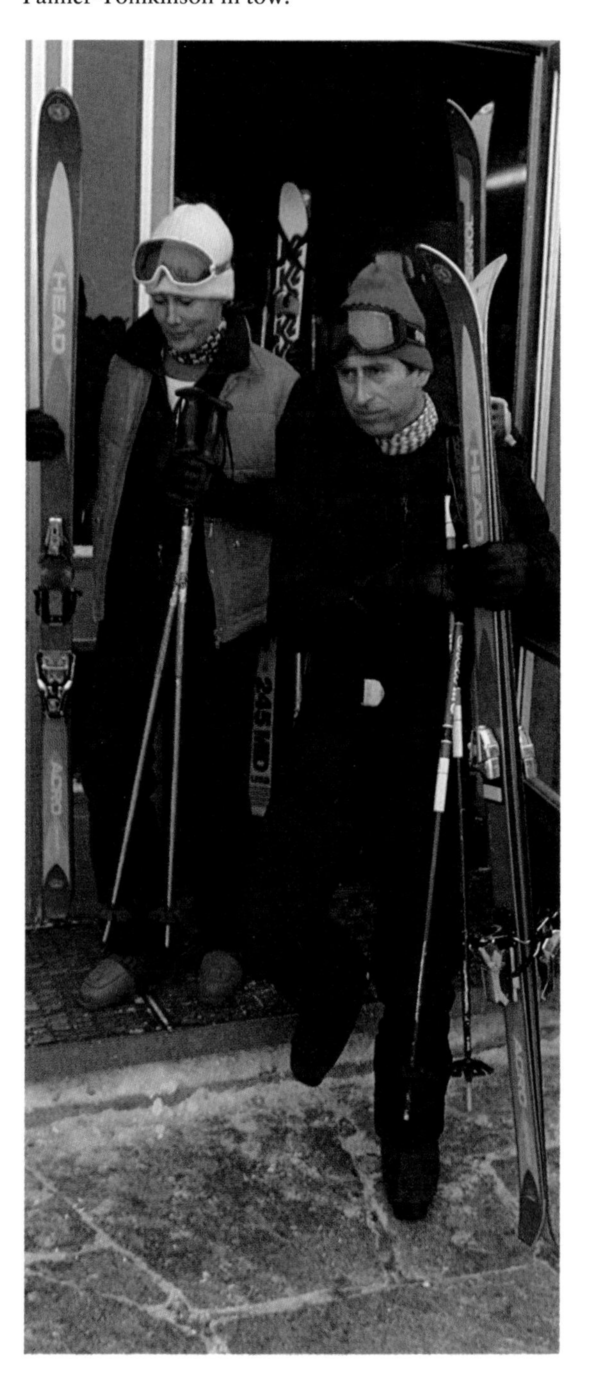

On 14 January I wrote a front-page story recording that Lady Diana and Prince Charles were together at Sandringham. It was planned that she should stay two or three days. In the event she stayed a hectic twenty-four hours and left by way of a back entrance while Prince Charles distracted our attention elsewhere. Nobody had seen her at any stage, but the pressure on the Queen and the rest of the Royal Family was so intense that it was ruining the holiday for everybody.

One of Prince Charles's detectives sought me out later on the same day to assure me that Lady Diana had now left and would I therefore agree to leave also. I said I would, but only if I could be given an assurance that Lady Diana would not be back. The detective, Jim McMaster, would not guarantee this, so I said that, in that case, I could not leave. Jim said he would take advice from the Prince and let me know. At lunchtime a message came back: 'You have Prince Charles's assurance that Lady Diana will not be back this weekend.' I immediately returned to London.

A few days later Prince Charles left on his annual skiing holiday for Klosters in Switzerland. Disappointed as she was, Diana did not accompany him. Both knew that the Prince would get no holiday at all if she was with him. For weeks Diana had looked forward to the trip and to using her own skiing skills, and at one stage she was quietly confident she'd be there. But after the troubles at Sandringham the writing was on the wall, and in the Tuesday *Daily Star*, before Prince Charles left for Switzerland, I revealed she would not be with him.

Just as sadly, I wasn't allowed to go on the trip either. It was agreed the Prince should be given a bit of peace.

On 2 February, Prince Charles returned to England, and two days later, as he admitted on his engagement day, 'I proposed to Diana.' She accepted him at once. But the news wasn't to creep out for another twenty-two days.

Charles and Diana had always been determined that nothing should get out before it was announced officially by Buckingham Palace, and they almost got away with it. Only a 'leak' from No. 10 Downing Street ruined their scheming, much to their fury. The top people's paper, *The Times*, were the lucky recipients of the news. And they threw it away by making the story about the third item of prominence on their front page.

But, before then, Diana had slipped away on holiday to Australia with her mother and stepfather, who have a farm at Yass in New South Wales. It was the last holiday with only her own family that she would ever have. She knew the storm that must erupt on her return in the wake of the engagement, and she wanted a period of peace to collect herself.

The entire ten days she was gone were something of a farce. I discovered almost immediately that she had disappeared and wrote a story saying she was on holiday in Australia. When her mother and stepfather were tackled about it, they lied and said that Diana was not with them. Explaining later that she had 'no regrets' about pretending that Lady Diana was not with her during their beach holiday, Mrs Shand Kydd said: 'I was determined to have what my daughter and I knew to be our last holiday together. I chose Australia because it's a country for which I have a great affection. The people there were marvellous – they succeeded in concealing us for ten days. A handful of very good friends arranged for us to have a holiday on the coast of New South Wales, just the two of us and my husband, in a private holiday house on the beach.

'We were just swimming and surfing – it was like a real family holiday. Of course, we talked about Diana's future life – I would be a very abnormal mother if we didn't. I enormously approve of my daughters marrying the men they love very much.'

On Diana's return to England – again amid great secrecy – there was one dreadful day that she had to get through before the announcement of the engagement. It happened on a Friday, just four days before 24 February.

Clearly confident that the usual press corps were well out of harm's way covering Prince Andrew's twenty-first birthday at Culdrose in Cornwall, Diana arrived at Nick Gaselee's training yard by car, sitting alongside Prince Charles. It was a cheeky assumption, and a wrong one. I'd had a tip at midnight that the two might be together, and had got up at 3 a.m. to drive to Lambourn, timing my arrival with theirs. It was my duty to check Highgrove on the way – where I was temporarily arrested by a policeman wondering who I was – and I therefore arrived five minutes after them. Not that it mattered. They were together, even though they kept well apart.

Within minutes their joyful reunion was ending in tears and misery. As Lady Diana was watching Prince Charles put Allibar through his paces on the gallops that morning, the horse collapsed and died of a massive heart attack. As the Prince quickly jumped off to cradle the horse's head in his arms, a weeping Lady Diana rushed to help. There was nothing she could do. Some time later both Charles and Diana returned to the Gaselee's house for breakfast.

Both were stony-faced and non-communicative, but since we were still unaware of the tragedy that had just taken place, we did not think too much about it. It was freezing cold, we were all starving, and to pass the time away while waiting outside the Gaselee home, we joked and chatted away ourselves. At times we may have been too noisy.

We were certainly shattered when we learned some time later of what had happened to Allibar. My first thought was that both the Prince and Lady Diana must think us incredibly callous for saying nothing when they finally emerged – again separately. I brooded on it and, the following Sunday, while at home, felt I ought to explain. I rang Diana at her flat and said how terribly sorry I was at the death of

Lady Diana's mother, Countess Spencer, on her wedding day in 1954.

Allibar and what an awful experience it must have been for her. I also explained that we had no idea that the horse was dead while we were waiting outside Mr Gaselee's home.

Lady Diana seemed grateful to hear it. She said: 'I couldn't believe you did know.'

I then said that I wanted to write to Prince Charles to say how sorry I was, but was reluctant since he might take my letter the wrong way. I didn't want him to feel that I was trying to curry favour.

Lady Diana replied: 'Mr Whitaker, he wouldn't think that. The fact that you want to take the trouble to write would mean everthing. Please do write to him,' she continued. 'He would really appreciate it. He certainly won't take it the wrong way.'

We then went on to chat about Diana's Australian holiday, to talk about my forthcoming visit there (on part of Prince Charles's tour down under in March and April) and many other topics. Towards the end of our conversation I asked how she was and when the great announcement would be. She laughed, said she was very well and reminded me of my advice to her a long time before about not answering my own questions.

I replied: 'Yes, but this is different now. Something has got to happen soon.'

She riposted: 'No, I'm not going to say anything else. Just go away and write that letter.'

I put the telephone down, not realizing this was the last time I would ever by able to ring her at home and find her picking up the phone herself. I had always been able to do so before. But Diana knew it would never happen again. Her final words of that conversation were, 'Good-bye, Mr Whitaker, and thank you.'

I sometimes wonder whether the engagement annoucement was possibly brought forward by a week or two, or even by a couple of months. It was strange for Diana to have told me in that final telephone call that she 'would be back at the kindergarten on Tuesday'. There was no reason for her to tell a lie. She didn't have to volunteer anything on the subject.

I do know that, with Prince Charles's trip to New Zealand, Australia and the United States not too far away, he wanted to make an announcement and then give himself some time before 'disappearing to the other side of the world for five weeks'. He has also since explained that, if the engagement hadn't happened when it did, it might not have been possible to make an announcement until his return from abroad in May, which would have meant a cold winter wedding; something he wanted to avoid.

And later, when I talked to Diana's flatmates, they admitted that they didn't realize it was to be made official on 24 February. I believe it is quite possible that it was literally a last-minute decision.

Anyway, little realizing that the engagement was only forty-one hours from being made official, I sat down and wrote to Prince Charles about the death of Allibar. The following day I hand-delivered the letter to Buckingham Palace at the side door where all communications are received after-hours. If I had gone to the other side of the Palace I would have seen Lady Diana's Mini Metro parked in the Buckingham Palace forecourt. If, if, if . . .

As a result of that urging from Lady Diana, however, I received a letter from Prince Charles that I will treasure for ever:

Dear Mr Whitaker,

I was *most* touched to receive your very kind and understanding letter. It was altogether a miserable business as I had become very fond of that old horse and the prospects were so exciting for the future . . . However, fate intervenes in strange ways.

Thank you so much for writing as you did.

Yours sincerely

Charles

The letter was handwritten and was dated 24 February 1981. He had taken the trouble to write on the very day he became engaged! But that was not the only occasion when HRH had personally demonstrated what a fine and understanding person he is.

In January 1980, while in Klosters, Switzerland, my wife, Iwona, had fallen badly while skiing. As she was being taken off the mountainside in a 'blood wagon' Prince Charles saw what had happened and that night wrote to her and had the letter dropped in at our hotel:

Dear Mrs Whitaker,

I was very sorry to discover that the figure I saw in the sledge this afternoon was you. What miserable bad luck to put yourself out of action like that. I do hope they look after you well in Klosters and that you will make a speedy recovery. With my best wishes – Charles.

My wife had, in fact, badly broken her knee in two places, and it was some time before she recovered. But as Iwona lay in hospital near by at Davos after a lengthy and painful operation, that note from HRH was a great comfort to her.

All day on Monday, 23 February, there had been rumours and more rumours that there was to be an engagement announcement at any time. I even received a telephone call from Germany asking whether I could confirm that it would be 'tomorrow' (Tuesday, 24 February) a story that they (the Germans) believed to be true.

I couldn't. The days had long gone when I wanted to write any more stories beginning 'Speculation mounted last night' . . . It was too late for all of that. If one was going to run a story, it had to be a lot more definite and it had to have names in it, not anonymous court officials, close friends or any other such euphemisms. I agreed with my paper that I shouldn't write, and that seemed to be the general view in Fleet Street.

But, even as I was delivering my letter on one side of Buckingham Palace, two freelance photographers were on the Constitution Hill side taking pictures of Lady Diana with her Mini Metro. They subsequently went to the *Sun* and sold them for a fee of several thousand pounds. And in the early hours of the following morning I knew the worst. The *Sun* had pictures of the Mini Metro in the Buckingham Palace forecourt and a story saying 'speculation grew last night . . .', reporting that Lady Diana was at the Palace.

But, far, far worse, *The Times* had its front-page story, casually headlined, 'Engagement of Prince to be announced today.' No rumour, no speculation, no guess work, just a cool, factual announcement. What is more, they got it right. Three days earlier I had sworn: 'If *The Times* ever scoops me I shall resign.' Happily, my editor never heard me say it.

Early that Tuesday morning I rang Diana at her flat. Anne Bolton answered and said she didn't know where Diana was and didn't know when she would be back. She added ominously: 'She hasn't been here all night.'

I went down to Coleherne Court anyway, and then on to Diana's kindergarten school, because Diana had told me in our Sunday telephone conversation that she would be back at school 'on Tuesday'.

It had been a lie – the only time in five and a half months that she had told a calculated untruth. At school they didn't know anything and were not expecting Diana. The only thing to do was to go to the Foreign and Commonwealth Office where Prince Charles was due at 10 a.m. I found the place was milling with reporters, photographers and television crews.

At one minute past ten the final proof that the announcement was about to be given became apparent. A spokeman came out and stated that the Prince's visit had been 'postponed'.

That was it, then. And at 11 a.m. the news became official.

Under the Royal Marriage Act of 1772, formal approval of the wedding had to be given by the Privy Council, for under the Act there is a provision that certain descendants of King George II cannot marry without the previous consent of the Sovereign signified under the Great Seal and declared in Council.

Both the Queen and Prince Charles, who are Privy Councillors, were at the meeting on 27 March in the White Drawing Room at Buckingham Palace, while Lady Diana, who isn't a Privy Councillor, was not. Those who did attend included the Prime Minister, Margaret Thatcher, the Opposition leader, Michael Foot, and the former Prime Ministers Harold Macmillan and Sir Harold Wilson. The Archbishop of Canterbury, Dr Robert Runcie, was also present. In fact the Queen simply dispensed with the formalities by using the solitary word 'consent'. After that, and to celebrate the event, she posed for the first official pictures with Prince Charles and Lady Diana on either side of her.

For once, Lady Diana looked slightly self-conscious about her 5 feet 8½ inches, and bent her knees slightly to reduce her height.

I remember the moment when the news came. I felt flat. Somehow I couldn't comprehend that five and a half months of non-stop work and beavering was ended. The game had been played and won.

But this mood didn't last long. There were the parents to be talked to, there were background stories to be written, and there was the interview with the happy couple to be listened to.

It was a Press Association reporter, Grania Forbes, who had this privilege. In fact she insisted on 'coming back to work for the day' to do it, despite being on maternity leave and very heavily pregnant. Grania's interview was printed on page 3 of the *Daily Star*:

> 'Prince Charles revealed yesterday how he popped the question to Lady Di – over dinner in his private sitting room at Buckingham Palace just before she flew off to Australia.
>
> 'I chose the moment so that she would have plenty of time to think about it,' he said. 'To decide if it was all going to be too awful.'
>
> And they made light of the difference in their ages – Prince Charles is 32 and Lady Di just 19. She said simply, 'The gap just does not matter.' But she admitted that in the past she had 'always ganged up with Prince Andrew'.
>
> And Charles added: 'Diana will certainly keep me young. You are only as old as you think you are.'

Though they have moved in the same circles for many years, the couple first became aware of each other at a shoot in November 1977, the Queen's Jubilee Year. 'We met in the middle of a ploughed field,' laughed Lady Di.

Prince Charles said: 'I remember a very jolly and amusing and bouncy 16-year-old. She was very attractive.'

And Lady Diana's first impression of Prince Charles? 'Pretty amazing,' she said.

Romance blossomed when Lady Diana went to Balmoral last July to help her sister Lady Jane with her first baby. 'We began to realize there was something in it', said Prince Charles. And he revealed that Lady Diana returned late in the year to Scotland to stay at the Queen Mother's home, Birkhall, to be near the Prince.

'The whole thing was planned like a military operation,' he said. And the Prince spoke of the problems they had in trying to conduct their courtship with the eyes of the world's press on them 'I rang up Diana on one occasion in Australia and they said she was not taking any calls,' he went on. 'I said, "It's the Prince of Wales speaking". But they said, "How do I know it's the Prince of Wales?" '

Eventually he had to ring another number before he was able to speak to his bride-to-be. Lady Diana smiled and said: 'It has been worthwhile, I think I coped all right.'

Of their engagement Prince Charles said: 'We have had to sit on it for three weeks – which hasn't been easy. I was determined it was going to be a secret.'

Discussing how much still had to be sorted out Prince Charles said they still hadn't decided where they would live after the wedding. He went on: 'I only have two rooms and a bedroom at the Palace so it will obviously be difficult to stay here for very long.' Their main base will be at his Gloucestershire home, Highgrove.

Asked if she had got the house organzed Lady Diana said with a grin: 'Not quite yet.' And the Prince added. 'It's just like camping. We've only got one room decorated downstairs and the bedroom organized. Otherwise everything is being painted. There's nothing there yet – no curtains, carpets or furniture – nothing.'

The Prince went on to point out that both of them loved the country and he would prefer to spend much more time there. The Prince went on to say he thought Lady Diana would make a very good Princess of Wales – 'I am sure she will be very, very good.'

Prince Charles and Lady Diana at Balmoral.

Charles and Diana meet their future neighbours at Tetbury, Gloucestershire.

Prince Charles and Lady Diana felt they both had a lot in common. 'Diana is a great outdoor-loving sort of person,' he said. Lady Diana added: 'We both love music and dancing and we both have the same sense of humour.' 'You'll definitely need that,' said the Prince with a laugh.

Grania noted that Lady Diana, proudly displaying her £28,000 diamond and sapphire ring from Garrards, seemed poised and confident as she sat beside her Prince. But she conceded it was 'marvellous' to have his moral support. 'It's always nice when there are two of you and there's someone there to help you,' she said.

On the television interview, the final question was, 'Are you in love?' The Prince said, 'Yes, whatever that may mean.' Lady Diana said, 'Of course.'

The public admission of when they had first met was not the same one Lady Diana had given me during our midnight chat outside her flat in December. Then she had said. 'I don't in fact remember a great deal about our first meeting, but it was when I was still wearing nappies.' On that occasion she had gone on wistfully: 'It's funny, but a lot of the best things happened when I was in nappies. It just seems to have been a good time of my life.'

Changing her mood, she then recalled that she and the Prince had been constant, regular friends ever since. 'I have known him all my life,' she had gone on. 'He was just somebody who was always around.'

And there was something else in the official interview that didn't tally with what I had always been told by Diana's friends: that originally she was concerned at the difference in their ages. Maybe, by the end, she wasn't, but both she and the Prince talked it over many times. And even now, with him already going thin on top, it must be something they both think about.

That engagement day I also recalled some of the many telephone conversations I had had with Diana over the months. One in particular had been most relevant, in which she had been asked why she was different from the Prince's previous girl friends. She said: 'Why has such a fuss been made of me? Do you and your colleagues think that I am the right person for him just because I don't have a past? Is it only really because I don't have a record of jumping in and out of bed with boy friends? What makes me so different?'

I remember replying at the time: 'There are many, many reasons why so many people want you to marry him.' Then I asked her a question. 'If you were to walk into a room in which you were alone with the Queen, the Duke of Edinburgh and the Prince of Wales, would that make you a little nervous?'

'No,' she said immediately. 'Why should it?'

I didn't need to say any more.

At the precise hour of the official announcement, two Scotland Yard detectives went to Lady Diana's flat in Coleherne Court (although, of course, she wasn't there) and stood guard. Diana herself was never to sleep at Coleherne Court again. Instead, for the first four days, she went to live at Clarence House, the London residence of the Queen Mother. There she had the comfort and peace that she needed in the midst of so much excitement.

She also had the friendship of a wise and worldly woman who was not only her grandmother's best friend but who also 'knew the royal ropes'. If Diana needed any royal coaching – which I have never believed she did – then who better to instruct her than the Queen Mum.

But, contrary to popular belief, she didn't stay at Clarence House for long and was soon off to stay with her sister, Lady Jane Fellowes, at their Kensington Palace home. She virtually made this address her base until the wedding.

One day, of course, she will live at Clarence House permanently. There is no doubt the Prince and Princess of Wales will inherit the place on the death of the Queen Mother. It should be whispered very softly, but, when the time comes, I hear that they also want Birkhall in Scotland as their own.

Many people had many things to say on that engagement day. Her father, Earl Spencer, and his wife Raine were deliriously happy at the news. I went to see them at their Grosvenor Square flat within minutes of the oficial announcement.

He told me how Prince Charles had telephoned him at his London flat and said: 'Can I marry your daughter? I have asked her and very surprisingly she has said yes.' The Earl said he told Charles: 'I am delighted. Well done.' Later that day Lord Spencer added cheekily: 'I wonder what he would have done if I had said no.'

Big sister Lady Sarah was equally happy. She boasted: 'I introduced them. I am Cupid. It is wonderful news and I am delighted.' She went on: 'The only difficult bit has been keeping quiet in the last ten days. I saw Diana in her London flat and I guessed when I saw her face. She was totally radiant, bouncing, bubbling, and I said, 'You're engaged,' and she said , 'Yes'. She just told me that they are getting

Paul Officer escorts Lady Diana as she leaves Coleherne Court for the last time, bound for Clarence House.

Lord Spencer on the day the engagement was announced.

married in the summer. They are both over the moon. He met Miss Right and she met Mr Right.'

On the question of the wedding date, July was chosen because Prince Charles 'can't bear' late autumn weddings when it is so cold. He was also insistent that the wedding should be in St Paul's Cathedral and not Westminster Abbey because 'the Cathedral is big enough to take one orchestra if not two.' He had long chats with Diana about the day, and both agreed they wanted the service to be 'a great musical occasion'.

But there was another reason why Westminster Abbey was rejected. It was first revealed to me by Lord Spencer on the day of the engagement. While sitting in his beautiful drawing room he suddenly said: 'I hope they won't marry at the Abbey. It has such unhappy memories.'

I asked what he meant. Lord Spencer started to explain that his first marriage (which had ended in divorce) had been at the Abbey, and that Earl Mountbatten had had his funeral service there, but then his wife, Raine, came flying across the room to interrupt. 'Do be quiet,' she said to Lord Spencer. 'Now, Mr Whitaker, we don't want anything like that appearing tomorrow to spoil the day, do we?'

I agreed not to write the story that day, but never promised not to do so in the future. So when, later on, it was announced that the ceremony was to be at St Paul's, I felt free to explain why.

The decision to hold Britain's wedding of the decade at St Paul's hid, I wrote, a secret sadness for Prince Charles and Lady Di. Buckingham Palace said officially that the cathedral was chosen for the ceremony on 29 July because it could accommodate more guests than Westminster Abbey. But the real reason for the break with tradition was, I knew, far more personal. Quite simply, the Abbey held too many unhappy memories for the Prince and his bride-to-be.

Lord Spencer had actually told friends: 'I hate the place. I never wanted Diana to marry there.' But the switch to St Paul's naturally left Abbey officials sad and disappointed. All major weddings this century have been held in Westminster Abbey, including those of the Queen, the Queen Mother, Princess Anne, Princess Margaret and Princess Alexandra. It seemed inconceivable that Prince Charles could marry anywhere else.

The Dean of Westminster must have realized there was a change on the cards when there was no approach from the Palace following the engagement.

The Spencers outside the family home, Althorp.

The Very Rev. Dr Edward Carpenter said: 'We are naturally disappointed that the marriage won't take place here. But we respect the couple's wishes and send them all our prayers for a happy day.'

But the switch was going to add considerably to the cost of the lavish ceremony, and the thought of so much splendour amid the gloom of Britain's economic crisis had been worrying the Royal Family. They didn't want the ceremony to look too extravagant. During the discussions between the Lord Chamberlain's Office, the Queen, Lady Diana Spencer and Prince Charles over whether the switch to St Paul's was really practical there was one delightful exchange.

Pressure was definitely put on Prince Charles not to forsake Westminster Abbey. He was urged to 'think again, if, for no other reason, than that we are worried that we will not have enough soldiers to line the route properly'.

With his typical quizzical look the Prince replied: 'Well, stand them further apart.'

A quite ludicrous 'message' was given to Lady Diana at that time from an entirely different quarter. Predictably, it came from the Communist-controlled *Morning Star* newspaper under a hilarious headline which said 'Don't do it, Lady Diana':

Lady Diana Spencer is to sacrifice her independence to a domineering layabout for the sake of a few lousy foreign holidays. As the future Queen of England she can expect a fair bit of first-class travel and a lot of attention, but with a £100,000 home of her own and a steady job as an exclusive nursery nurse, who needs it?

Morning Star readers may find it hard to sympathize with the daughter of a millionaire earl with a Buckingham Palace future. But the 'suitable bride' treatment she has received at the hands of the press and even her own family degrades not only her, but all women.

Most obnoxious have been the delicate assurances of her virginity. Any illusions Lady Diana may have about being a person, the owner of her own body and sexuality, should have been sharply shattered by her father and uncle who have publicly guaranteed their valuable commodity will be delivered to the Prince in a state of unsullied innocence.'

The article quoted Harold Brooks-Baker, managing director of *Debrett* as saying: 'The Lady Diana will bring back Stuart blood to the Royal Family. The Prince of Wales's bride had to be someone acceptable to this country, his family and who was young enough to have a large number of children if necessary, and whose history was impeccable.'

The *Morning Star* article sniffed: 'Perhaps we are carping, but surely even she deserves to be regarded with more dignity than a pedigree Fresian cow.'

The time of the engagement produced many light moments. Another came while waiting for the wedding to take place when Prince Charles – obviously irritated at Diana's pedigree being for ever trotted out – commented acidly: 'I am getting fed up learning all about her past. I am beginning to think she is more Royal than I am.'

One thing I found sad was the fact that, when it came to choosing bridesmaids, none of Lady Diana's flatmates were picked. If ever three girls had shown total loyalty and devotion to one of their number they were Virginia, Anne and Carolyn. They were almost the first to be told about the engagement, and for three weeks had kept quiet even though they must have been bursting at times to spread the news.

Three days after the engagement I called round to see them all to talk about the excitement of the week and to find out how long they had known. I then asked which of them would be bridesmaids. Carolyn just shrugged her shoulders. She didn't know. There had hardly been chance to talk to Diana since the engagement day. But when the list was released in the second week of April, none of them got a mention. In fact, neither did many other friends of Diana, even though, of course, she knew all the attendants who had been selected.

In the list of five bridesmaids, the one she loved best was Clementine Hambro, a pretty five-year-old girl whom Diana had taught at kindergarten, and who is a great-granddaughter of Sir Winston Churchill. Clementine, we were told, became Diana's darling at the London nursery school. When asked what she thought about the honour, Clementine, speaking from her New York home, said: 'Miss Diana was my favourite teacher and I was sad when she had to leave to marry Prince Charles. But I am glad to be a bridesmaid for her.'

The other bridesmaids, with the exception of Sarah Gaselee (the ten-year-old daughter of Nick Gaselee) were far more predictable and regally trained. Chief bridesmaid was to be the seventeen-year-old Lady Sarah Armstrong-Jones, daughter of Princess Margaret and Prince Charles's great friend Lord Snowdon, who was asked to do the official engagement pictures. Others chosen were Lord Mountbatten's granddaughter, India Hicks, and six-year-old Catherine Cameron, whose mother, Lady Cecil, was one of Prince Charles's old flames.

The two pages chosen were again predictable: Lord Nicholas Windsor, the eleven-year-old son of the Duke of Kent, and Edward van Cutsem, aged eight, the son of the Prince's old friend Hugh van Cutsem, whose own father had been a famous Newmarket trainer.

The loyal flatmates on whom Diana had leaned so much must have felt disappointed even though they would never admit to it.

Although it appears that Diana was prepared to go along with the choice of others on the selection of the bridesmaids and page boys, it is unlikely that she will give way so easily on other matters as her marriage proceeds. Anybody who gives the Prince the nickname 'Fishface' and uses it to him is someone with whom to be reckoned. She has plenty of fire and nerve about her, and I am confident that, with her native charm – at times cunning – she will win her way on many decisions. She is very much her own woman and will *never* allow herself to become anybody's doormat.

But it is the caring, loving, vulnerable touch that helps to give Lady Diana so much warmth, as has been demonstrated many times since February. There was the occasion when the tears came to her eyes as she saw Prince Charles off at Heathrow before his plane took him round the world and away from her arms for five weeks. The hearts of women everywhere must have gone out to her in that parting. She was in love, and she didn't want him to be going away for so long. Maybe royals shouldn't cry in public, but she didn't care about protocol in that instant.

There was then the time when the Dean Close, Cheltenham schoolboy looked into Diana's eyes and said, 'May I kiss the hand of my future Queen?' and she replied, 'Of course you may.' Many more people succumbed to her charms that day, especially when she added to the boy: 'You will never be able to live this down.'

And then, twice, within the space of a week in March, she had to endure the anxiety of Prince Charles being thrown from his racehorse, Good Prospect, first at Sandown, where she was in the stand, and then at Cheltenham, where she was absent. It was not that she was frightened for the Prince on these two occasions, but the concern showed clearly in her eyes.

On the other hand, her independence was well demonstrated – I personally thought to an exaggerated degree – when she attended her first official engagement with Prince Charles: a poetry reading evening at the Goldsmith's Hall in the City of London. The dress she picked was so low cut that it was almost possible to see her tummy button when she leant forward as she stepped out of her limousine. It was clearly her way of telling the world: 'This is me, Diana Spencer. I'm not just the fiancée of the Prince of Wales.' There were gasps from the crowd as she struggled to keep up the top of the black silk taffeta dress, with nothing to rely on except a prayer and a lot of will-power.

It was all splendid and deliciously independent, but Diana didn't look too comfortable. The dress was too distantly removed from those high-cut Edwardian numbers which she always wore before her engagement. They had been much more her style. The new dress simply didn't suit her. It was as simple as that. Another guest that evening was Princess Grace of Monaco. She looked duly amused.

But Diana was obviously happy enough with it, for the very next day it was announced that its designers – David and Elizabeth Emanuel – were to make her wedding dress. Every other designer in England was consumed with envy.

David, twenty-eight, tall and trendy, and Elizabeth, twenty-seven, described the dress as 'the dress of the century that will never be sketched'. For security reasons, it was going to be far too dangerous to put the design on paper. Their staff were sworn to secrecy, and David declared: 'I am itching, it is all so exciting, we are so honoured to be doing it.'

The couple have made their name by using pure silk chiffons, silk taffeta, finest tulle and antique lace to create garments that are often worn over huge, stiff, net petticoats and which shimmer with delicate beadwork and sequins, as one fashion writer wrote.

Why so romantic, David was asked? He replied: 'One needs romance in the climate in which we live. To me, if there is the excuse to dress up, you should dress up. It is very sad not to bother. And for anyone who insists on being sloppy, well, then, she can dress down divinely.'

There was even a sensational suggestion at this stage that the dress for St Paul's might not be white. Said David: 'It might not be, you know. We did one in palest pink net which was fragile and delicate. It was absolutely beautiful.'

The Emanuels went to great lengths to get the dress right. They even went to St Paul's to 'study the background against which the dress will move'. Normally they take one month to make a wedding dress, but were grateful to have four months in which to prepare Diana's.

'Lady Diana's has to be perfect, and remember, we look after the total look,' explained David. 'We can tie up with a milliner [Frederick Fox, the Royal hatter], advise on hair [her hairdresser being Kevin Shanley of Headline in South Kensington], make-up, see that the flowers, shoes and just about everything are part of the finished picture'.

Kevin Shanley, who also does the hair of Lady Diana's two sisters, Lady Sarah and Lady Jane, was deservedly kept on by Lady Diana after the engagement. There was no reason to change. But he had no previous royal connections, and it could have happened. He was in fact the first 'outsider' to be told of the engagement when he learned, on the night of 23 February, that Diana wanted to come in early the next day. Kevin, who had been doing Diana's hair for five years, would never have dreamed of giving the secret away. Talking of that morning and all the excitement, he said: 'She walked in, waved a diamond and sapphire ring under my nose and said "What do you think of that?" We all stood around in amazement and wished her all the best.'

The only difference these days is that, instead of Lady Diana going to Kevin's salon, he now goes to her. Certainly what Kevin created has swept the hair-fashion world. The 'Lady Di' hairstyle has been copied on every continent, as Prince Charles found on his tour of New Zealand and Australia soon after the engagement. There were 'Lady Di lookalikes' on every corner.

Not a production line for Madame Tussaud's, but rather a parade of Lady Di look-alikes in Australia.

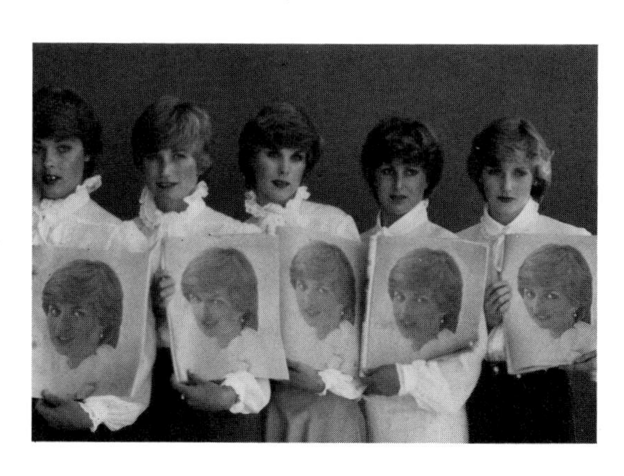

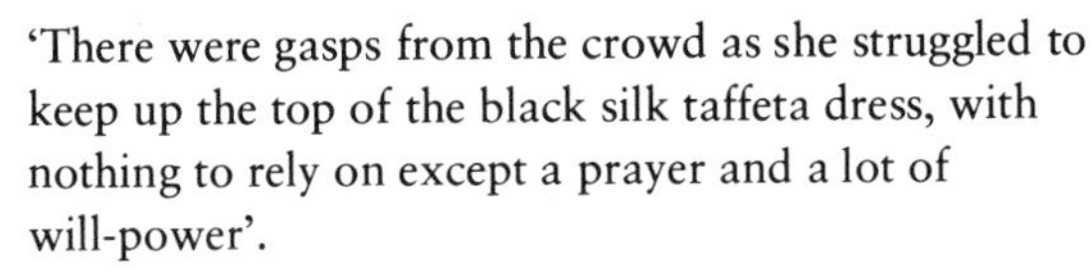

'There were gasps from the crowd as she struggled to keep up the top of the black silk taffeta dress, with nothing to rely on except a prayer and a lot of will-power'.

Above right: engagement day.

Shortly after the news of the wedding dress, Prince Charles had some of his own. It was announced that he would have two 'best men' – his two younger brothers, Prince Andrew and Prince Edward, with the elder one, Andrew, twenty-one, being in charge of the ring. The two were to be officially known as the bridegroom's supporters. The idea was in line with a royal custom going back into the last century. Edward VII, George V and George VI all had two supporters.

The tradition when a Prince of Wales marries is that the wedding ring be made of Welsh gold. And this one was made at Collingwoods, the Crown jewellers in Conduit Street, where Lady Diana was so anxious not to be photographed by Ken Lennox just before Christmas!

Other details to emerge were that Lady Diana would be given away by her father, Earl Spencer, and that the two would travel in the last of the four open carriages the two miles or so from Buckingham Palace. The first carriage in the procession would be for members of the Royal Family, including the Queen Mother, Princess Anne and Princess Margaret. The second carriage would contain the Queen. The third would transport Prince Charles.

At the end of the hour-long ceremony, conducted by the Archbishop of Canterbury, Dr Robert Runcie, and assisted by the Dean of St Paul's, the Very Rev. Alan Webster, the Prince and Lady Diana would lead a three-coach procession back to Buckingham Palace.

All this lay a very long way from the Scottish river bank near Balmoral where, months before, Diana had warily eyed me though her hand-held mirror. This July Day marked the end of a six-year chase. It was also a day for me to look forward to with great happiness. I had said many times to Diana: 'If he doesn't marry you, he is a fool.'

And the Prince of Wales is certainly nothing of the kind.

The Girls

The Girls

At times it was pure theatre. Prince Charles's love-life was certainly one of the longest-running shows that the West End or, indeed, any other End has ever witnessed. It was a production that any playhouse manager would have loved to have been able to put on. It was non-stop, it was exciting, it was unpredictable and sexy. There were moments of pure farce as one girl would exit left even as another was entering stage from the other side.

The list of leading ladies was long and varied. There were débutante types, Latin American beauties, horsey girls, actresses, pop singers, union leaders, and even perfectly ordinary girls whose fathers were dukes, earls or mere marquises.

Prince Charles was a late developer sexually. It is believed that not until he was nineteen and already at Trinity College, Cambridge, did he first make love to a girl. It is pure speculation as to whether this lucky girl was the exotically-named Lucia Santa Cruz, the daughter of the then Chilean Ambassador to London. But a suggestion a couple of years ago that she was indeed the one to introduce the heir to the throne to the delights of the bedroom has never been denied. It is traditional that the sons of the upper classes and, of course, the Royal Family be initiated by older women, and it seems certain that this is what happened in the case of Prince Charles.

Lucia, tall, dark-haired and oozing sex appeal, was three years older than the Prince when they got together at Cambridge. The Prince was reading history, Lucia was helping the Master of Trinity, Lord Butler, to research his political memoirs, *The Art of the Possible.* The story is told that Lord Butler slipped Lucia a key to the Master's Lodge so she and the Prince could be together, alone. Lord Butler is quoted as telling writer Tony Holden that he 'felt it his duty to help Prince Charles enjoy the dwindling days of as private a life as he would ever know'.

The former Tory Minister, a great personal friend of Prince Charles and a man who was once but a hairsbreadth away from becoming Leader of the Conservative party, has since denied that he 'slipped any key' to Lucia, but a letter is in existence saying: 'At the Prince's request, my wife and I allowed Lucia to stay in the Master's Lodge so that they could have more privacy.'

Lucia, like most of the Prince's previous girl friends, is now happily married. Her husband is a Chilean lawyer and they live in South America. Her 'reward' for everything she did for Prince Charles, and for never opening her mouth afterwards, is continuing friendship, a warm welcome whenever they see each other and an agreement by HRH to be a godfather to her first child.

Lucia may have been the first person to 'know' the Prince in the biblical sense, but there were plenty of others who were 'linked' with Charles before he became a man. The writers Graham and Heather Fisher not so long ago listed the number of girls who have, over the years, been put forward by newspapers and magazines as 'suitable brides'. The list, which ran to six pages, reached an amazing total of sixty, twenty of whom were princesses. And there have been more than a few added since.

But while writers and chroniclers of the Prince's sex-life may often have got carried away with their sometimes outrageous suggestions, the Prince himself did not help matters by being a self-confessed romantic who 'falls in love easily'. In a startling interview with me in 1978, Lady Diana's elder sister, Lady Sarah, admitted this to be the case. At the same time, she went on to say: 'I do not believe he wants to marry yet.'

It was around the same time that I discussed the subject of marriage with the Prince at a game of polo at Smith's Lawn on the day it was 'officially' announced that he was to marry Princess Marie-Astrid of Luxembourg.

Lucia Santa Cruz, allegedly 'the one to introduce the heir to the delights of the bedroom.'

He told me then: 'I have only just left the Navy and I am in no hurry at all to get married. I have not yet met the person I will wed.'

This wasn't in fact true, although the Prince cannot be blamed for making such a remark. Apart from meeting Lady Diana when she was a baby wearing nappies – an occasion that neither remembers too clearly – they had been reintroduced during November 1977 by Lady Sarah! That was six months before our conversation.

Prince Charles's earliest public date was with his cousin, Marilyn Wills, the daughter of the Queen's closest friends, John and Jean Wills. A lover of all things musical, the Prince and Marilyn chose to see the smash hit, *The Sound of Music*. He was aged fourteen and, however hard anybody looked, the two weren't caught holding hands once.

While at Gordonstoun, Prince Charles did not have any of the creature comforts supplied by the fairer sex that his younger brothers Andrew and Edward received when it was their turn to be educated at this tough Scottish school. Co-education had not been introduced into any public school on a wide scale at that time, and there is no doubt in my mind that, if girls had been at Gordonstoun with Prince Charles, he would have enjoyed his schooldays very much more.

But, despite this, he did have an encounter of a reasonably close kind when, at the age of seventeen, he was invited to attend the birthday party of Sandra Spence, the daughter of an Elgin solicitor. By all accounts, the party never had a chance of getting too far out of control. The Prince's detective stayed in the same room as everyone else for the entire evening and nobody dared to do anything. Rather unnecessarily Sandra said after the party: 'There was no necking or anything like that.'

Having a detective in close attendance remained a problem for Prince Charles – and his girl friends – for the rest of his bachelor days. Who can blame any girl for being 'put off' through knowing that a 'tec' is waiting outside while they are trying to have fun on the other side of the door?

One girl friend once told me: 'It is inhibiting enough being in an intimate situation with the heir to the throne without constantly thinking that you are keeping somebody waiting nearby.'

Detectives grow understandably nervous when 'the boss' is with somebody they are not totally sure about. The night can also become long and cold, waiting outside the flat of a girl who is receiving Prince Charles's charms. Detectives, particularly the not-so-regular ones, have been heard to complain that they wished he would 'get on with it'. But that isn't Prince Charles's style. He is in love with the idea of love. And that makes for a slow build-up.

The one thing he cannot stand is a flash, bang, wallop evening. HRH is a man who wooed with flowers, tender words, a lot of hand holding and soft candlelight. At the end of the evening he would drop off his girl friend at her flat and then get on the telephone to her as soon as he returned to his own apartment in Buckingham Palace. For the next hour he would talk softly and lovingly to the girl he had just been taking out. He would say how much he loved her, how much he would enjoy being married to her, how much he savoured the colour of her eyes, the smell of her hair.

And he wouldn't say all of this to them just for effect. He meant what he was saying, and most of the time the girls loved to hear it. But there were occasions when one or two of them were absolutely dying to get to sleep but didn't dare to end the conversation.

Prince Charles has never needed to say anything 'for effect'. It would take an exceptional girl not to be flattered by receiving the attention of Prince Charles. It would take incredible self-restraint to say 'No' to the Prince of Wales. In fact HRH is not a person to take advantage of his position when 'chatting up' ladies. The question of whether it is his position as the Prince of Wales or his own natural charm that makes girls interested in him is one that must often have worried him.

But there are two women – both married – who have, entirely though their own choice, wholeheartedly succumbed to the charm of Prince Charles. These are Lady Tryon, the Australian-born wife of one of the Prince's oldest friends, Lord Tryon (whose father was Treasurer to the Queen), and Camilla Parker-Bowles, whose husband, Andrew, is a serving cavalry officer.

Tony and Dale Tryon are two friends upon whom the Prince feels comfortable to call at any time. He does not feel that he has to give any warning, and Dale, in particular, welcomes this.

Privately, Dale admits that she loves the Prince dropping in. She is regarded as one of London's best hostesses, and this means that HRH lacks for nothing.

Says a friend: 'She's not a beauty in the true sense of the word, but she attracts men easily. Dustmen whistle at her, so do schoolboys. And she loves it.'

Says another friend: 'At school she had a large following. At the tram-stop when she got on there was always a crowd of about twenty schoolboys waiting for her. They would walk four or five stops just for the pleasure of seeing her and maybe sitting next to her on the tram.'

Dale has got a lovely sense of humour, too – also much appreciated by HRH. The evening she knew that she was pregnant not too long ago she said to her husband: 'I've got something to tell you, Ant.'

'Don't tell me you are having another baby,' replied Lord Tryon.

'Kanga'

'Anyway, give me a drink first.'

Said Dale. 'I think you'd better have two drinks. I'm having twins.'

Prince Charles is not expected to call upon Dale so often following marriage to Lady Diana, but old habits die hard for the Prince. He will always be grateful for the help he received while progressing from adolescence to full manhood and contact between Dale and Charles seems bound to continue.

HRH is godfather to the Tryon's son, also named Charles.

The Prince, who calls Lady Tryon 'Kanga' (short for kangaroo), was particularly grateful for help received when he was on his 1977 visit in November to Australia. She flew there to act as his official hostess. Some surprise was expressed about it at the time since it was not felt to be wholly necessary. But Kanga clearly enjoyed every minute of being with the Prince. And the feeling was fairly obviously reciprocated.

The other married woman in the life of Prince Charles – and one who has been even more constant in her attention – is dark-haired Camilla Parker-Bowles. She has looked after the Prince for much longer than Dale, and consequently is regarded even more affectionately.

She has constantly 'looked after' Charles and helped him to become the sort of man he is today. The Prince has been friendly with Camilla since the early 1970s when Andrew, now a colonel, was escorting both his wife-to-be and Lady Caroline Percy, a daughter of the Duke of Northumberland and, ironically, another old flame.

Camilla Parker-Bowles.

Lady Tryon

Anna Wallace.

Says a friend: 'It was amusing to watch Charles just beginning to feel his oats and red-blooded women really turned him on. He has never got out of the habit.'

It is interesting that older and married women have often excited members of the Royal Family.

Edward VII, when Prince of Wales, involved the monarchy in womanizing and even got involved in a divorce. Prince Charles has far too much a sense of duty to do anything so foolish, but, as with his great-uncle, the late Duke of Windsor, he has always felt comfortable with married women. They are no threat to him, they are not too demanding and he has always been able to relax in their company.

Camilla and Dale not only spent much of their time seeing that everything ran smoothly in the private life of their Prince, but were largely responsible for guiding Charles towards a person so eminently suitable as Lady Diana. They wanted to help the Prince to choose somebody like Diana, and to push what they considered undesirable people right out of the way.

If a girl wanted to get to the side of Prince Charles and stay there they had to get on with Dale and Camilla. There is no question but that Anna Wallace and these two never really got on and that didn't help her cause at all. A friend has described how Anna would argue with

them, resenting the influence they seemed to have over Prince Charles. 'She's tough girl, Anna, but in the end she realized that she would never be able to get these two on her side. Even then, she retained a hold on the Prince because he was so very much in love with her.'

When Prince Charles took up with Diana after his affair with Anna ended, both Camilla and Dale immediately approved the switch and did all they could to encourage the relationship. They gave their official seal of approval to the nineteen-year-old, and helped the true path of royal love to run smoothly. In the early days, Camilla and Andrew, who is in the Household Cavalry, often played host to the young couple.

It was in their Wiltshire home that the first seeds of love were nurtured. It was here that the first serious discussions of marriage were carried on. Diana is of course aware of the extent to which Camilla and Dale enjoy Charles's confidence and it is unthinkable that she would ever come to resent it.

Charles, in the one way he always shows his gratitude to his very closest married friends, is godfather to Thomas Parker-Bowles, age six.

Andrew, a former boy friend of Princess Anne, and Tony Tryon enjoy the proximity they have to the Prince. They find it flattering to be invited to Balmoral, Sandringham and Windsor Castle for weekends. They enjoy being friends with the Prince and like the thought that nobody is closer to the future King of England.

Camilla Parker-Bowles, 1965.

When married women appeared at the Prince's side it did not make the same sort of excitement in the press as when a new, unattached girl moved alongside him. The strain on these girls was often almost unbearable, and in many cases it put them off. No earlier girl was anywhere near being able to handle the media in the style Lady Diana showed.

The sort of well-brought-up girls with whom Prince Charles tended to mix fairly naturally hated the attention of photographers and reporters. In fairness to Prince Charles, he would warn them what was likely to happen. He would tell them that, if the pressure became too great, they should approach palace officials for assistance. Often they couldn't or wouldn't and simply fled – into the arms of somebody else. The list, as the years went by and the Prince flitted from one girl to the next, grew longer and longer. It depressed Prince Charles unutterably at times. But his views on marriage were that it had to be exactly right.

At various times he said: 'I will not become a martyr to the cause', and 'Whenever I give a dinner party these days more and more of the people seem to be married.'

In one famous interview, in the mid 1970s, he talked at length about the whole subject: 'Marriage is a much more important business than falling in love. I think one must concentrate on marriage being essentially a question of mutual love and respect for each other.

'Creating a secure family unit in which to bring up children, to give them a happy, secure upbringing – that's what marriage is all about, creating a home. Essentially, you must be good friends, and love, I'm sure, will grow out of that friendship.' Which in my opinion, is exactly what happened in his relationship and growing love for Lady Diana.

'I have', he continued, 'a particular responsibility to ensure that I make the right decision. The last thing I could possibly entertain is getting divorced. I've fallen in love with all sorts of girls and I fully intend to go on doing so. But I've made sure I haven't married the first person I've fallen in love with.'

Then came the famous quote:

And then there was Sybilla Dorman

'The right age for marriage is around thirty. By this time you have seen a great deal of life, met a large number of girls, been able to see what types of girls there are, fallen in love every now and then and you know what it's all about.'

Later, the Prince talked about the sort of girl he might marry.

'You have to remember that when you marry in my position you're going to marry someone who, perhaps, is one day going to be Queen. You've got to choose somebody very carefully I think, who could fulfil this particular role, and it has got to be somebody pretty unusual.

'The one advantage about marrying a princess, for instance, or somebody from a royal family, is that they do know what happens.'

But in those early teenage days, marriage was a million miles from the Prince's mind as he set off on the long romantic road to the High Altar of St Paul's Cathedral.

I suppose his first real girl friend was Sybilla Dorman, daughter of Malta's Governor-General, Sir Maurice Dorman. They met at Cambridge at around the time of the Prince's liaison with Lucia Santa Cruz while both were reading history. Sybilla invited HRH to holiday with her in Malta.

It was noted by the accompanying press corps at the time that they spent a part of their vacation rubbing sun-tan oil on to each other. That, added to the fact that Sybilla had been invited on board the Royal Yacht following the Investiture ceremony in Wales, caused much comment. But nothing permanent looked like emerging from this friendship and Sybilla came to be happily married to somebody else.

A colonel's daughter, Rosie Clifton, was another who fitted in to the category of a girl who went out with the Prince briefly before moving on and marrying elsewhere. Rosie was a regular escort of the Prince in the autumn of 1973. It was said at the time that she must care a lot forCharles because she picnicked with him in freezing cold weather during a grouse shoot.

The harsh fact is that anybody who joins the Royal Family on shooting days in Scotland is liable to end up frozen to the marrow. They are *all* expected to eat out in the open, whatever the weather conditions. That is the way in which the Queen and her family enjoy themselves!

. . . and Cindy Buxton

Rosie, pretty, slim and with a pair of legs that would do credit to a Bluebell girl, is now married to Mark Vestey, a polo-playing pal of Prince Charles and the younger brother of the meat baron, Lord 'Sam' Vestey.

Another girl friend of this period was Lucinda Buxton, one of the daughters of Aubrey Buxton, the television chief and naturalist friend of Prince Philip. Prince Charles took her to a Trinity May Ball. They had a few more dates, but soon were parted, and the doors then opened again and again for a whole procession of nymphets to move in Charles's direction.

The list of girls who paraded before the Prince over the next ten years or so was as impressive as it was fantastic. Most were very pretty, many were completely suitable, others were no more than passing fancies as the Prince followed his self-confessed desire of 'falling in love' many times before even considering that one day he might actually have to settle down.

Most of the girls would warrant a whole page to themselves in a society book. And, to be fair, most would have made a pretty good job of being Queen one day. But none had that vital ingredient for which the Prince was looking. It could have been that everybody was too young at the time they were dating. But none of these 'affairs' were a waste on either side, and nearly all the girls from these years have since married.

The list included Lady Leonora Grosvenor, daughter of the Duke of Westminster, who is now wife to the Earl of Lichfield; her younger sister, Lady Jane Grosvenor, now the Duchess of Roxburghe; and the two Roman Catholic daughters of the Duke of Northumberland, Lady Victoria Percy and Lady Caroline Percy. Lady Victoria is now married to a landowner, John Cuthbert, while Lady Caroline married the Spanish horticulturist, Count Pierre de Cabarrus, in January 1974.

Other dates included Bettina Lindsay, Lord Balniel's flaxen-haired daughter, of whom the Prince was said to be 'very fond'. The two met at the home of the Marquis of Salisbury, and Bettina was then invited to stay at both Balmoral and Windsor. But the romance cooled when Bettina went to study in Paris; she is now Mrs Peter Drummond-Hay. Then there was Lady Cecil Kerr, daughter of the Marquis of Lothian, now married to Donald Cameron of Lochiel; Lady Henrietta Fitzroy, daughter of the Duke of Grafton, married to a lawyer, Edward St George, who is twenty years older than Etta, as the Prince called her.

. . . and Bettina Lindsay

. . . and Lady Jane Grosvenor

. . . and Angela Nevill

And so the list continues: Lady Charlotte Manners, daughter of the Duke of Rutland, one of the very few still unmarried; her cousin Elizabeth 'Libby' Manners, until recently the sweetheart of the Marquis of Blandford, the heir to the Dukedom of Marlborough; Angela Nevill, the daughter of Prince Philip's private secretary and one of his oldest and most trusted friends, Lord Rupert Nevill, who is another one still unmarried; Louise Astor, beautiful daughter of Lord Astor of Hever, who in August 1979 married David Herring, the brother of Jane Ward.

To complete this particular list we might add Georgiana Russell, daughter of the British diplomat Sir John Russell, who is now the wife of a Welsh landowner, Mr Brooke Boothby; Caroline Longman, daughter of the famous publisher, Mark Longman, who died recently and who is another who currently remains unmarried. And there was Lady Camilla Fane, the beautiful daughter of the Earl of Westmorland, the Queen's Master of the Horse.

Lady Camilla Fane and Lady Sarah Spencer were Royal Ascot week guests of the Queen in the year, 1977, when it was announced that the Prince was 'to marry' Princess Marie-Astrid. Camilla went to watch the Prince play polo after racing, but after that week she was not seen publicly in his company again. It is possible that her friendship with a cockney car dealer, George Wright (who subsequently committed suicide), was something which did not help with maintaining a close friendship with the Prince.

During this period, however, there was also a different 'list' – one which included girls who were far more important in forming the character of Prince Charles. They were more important because they became much closer to Charles.

. . . and Georgiana Russell

. . . and Caroline Longman

. . . and Camilla Fane

One of the earliest was Laura Jo Watkins, the glossy blonde-haired daughter of an American rear-admiral. Prince Charles met her at San Diego, California, when he called in there while serving aboard HMS *Jupiter.* For one whole week, during that courtesy call, she seemed to be at every function where the Prince was present. The American press, continually making reference back to the Duke of Windsor, was put in mind of the American double-divorcee, Wallis Simpson.

When, back in England, Prince Charles made his maiden speech in the House of Lords, Laura Jo was in the Strangers' Gallery to hear him. She seemed happy, in fact a good deal too happy, to be associated with Charles, and that didn't go down at all well.

The week-end after the Prince's speech, larger than usual crowds turned up at Cowdray Park to watch him play polo. They weren't there to see the Prince clout a white ball around with a polo stick. They were there to witness the real thing. But everybody was disappointed. As Prince Charles told the eager photographers: 'You don't think I'm such a bloody fool as to bring her here today, do you?'

Laura Jo then disappeared for three years until, totally unexpectedly, she re-emerged at Deauville in the summer of 1978 when she flew with the Prince's polo friend, Captain Guy Wildenstein (son of the internationally known art dealer, Daniel Wildenstein) to France where, not surprisingly, she met the Prince again. That particular week-end, when the Prince was surrounded by some of the prettiest girls in the world, was a bit of a disaster.

...and Laura Jo Watkins

The Prince loves plenty of attention, but he loathed the way the American girl kept sweeping her hair from one side to the other, obviously posing. Nor did he like her affected voice, or the way she never stop chattering. But perhaps Laura Jo and the heir to the throne made it up when the official festivities of the night were finished and the two could get away together for an hour or so.

When I tackled Guy about how Laura Jo had happened to be in Deauville for the week-end, and who had made the decision to fly her over, he took all responsibility.

He said: 'I brought her here as a surprise for Prince Charles. After all, they are old friends.'

Guy, who knew Laura Jo from college in America, denied that he had sought Prince Charles's permission before making any moves. But I have since been told this is nonsense. Guy would never have dared to do what he did without getting approval from Prince Charles first. Perhaps it was all a mistake. Anyway, she never ever appeared again. As one close to the Prince told me at the time: 'Relax. The Prince enjoyed her company for a while but don't worry – that one has *no* chance of ever being Queen'.

Prince Charles's girl friends have often been dubbed 'Charlie's Angels', and one real one flitted around the Prince briefly at about this time. This particular Angel – from the television series – was Farrah Fawcett-Majors. The Prince had met her in Hollywood in 1977, and not long afterwards she arrived to do a charity show with Earl Mountbatten in aid of the Prince's much-loved United World Colleges. Embarrassingly, she gave several interviews professing her admiration for the Prince. After she returned home the two never met again.

Another uncomfortable moment for the Prince came after he had met Margaret Trudeau, who was then wife of the Canadian Prime minister, Pierre Trudeau. She gave an interview in which she said the Prince 'looked long and hard down my cleavage'. The royal silence that

. . . and Farrah Fawcett-Majors

. . . and Margaret Trudeau

. . . and Princess Caroline of Monaco

greeted this remark was deafening.

In fact, if the Prince ever had done such a thing it would have been directly against the advice of his father – advice that he has usually heeded. He once told the actress Susan Hampshire, in a line-up at a film première, that if ever he came across an actress wearing a very low-cut dress he had been warned by Prince Philip to look the person straight between the eyes.

One other brief and tricky relationship during this shaking-down period in the Prince's life was a friendship with the delicious Fiona Watson, daughter of the Steward of the Jockey Club and Yorkshire landowner, Lord Manton. First of all I discovered and subsequently wrote in the *Daily Express* William Hickey column that Fiona – under another name – had revealed all of her 38-23-35 figure in full and glorious colour across eleven pages of *Penthouse* magazine. Worse, her boy friend then started to complain about the Prince 'pinching my girl friend'.

It was enough to send everybody running for cover. But still the girls kept coming. There was even a brief and disastrous meeting with Princess Caroline of Monaco in 1977. For years these two royal superstars had been linked. Many believed that they were destined for each other, but nothing could have been further from the truth.

It seemed unbelievable to many people, including most in my own profession of journalism, that when Charles and Caroline finally got together in Monte Carlo far a charity evening it was the very first time they had met. And neither particularly liked what they saw. She was 'bored' by his squareness and conservatism, he 'irritated' by her flippancy and the fact that she was forty-five minutes late for their meeting.

Prince Charles later commented: 'Before I arrived the world had me engaged to Caroline. With our first meeting the world had us married – and now the marriage is already in trouble.'

When Princess Caroline began her disastrous marriage to Philippe Junot in 1978, the Prince refused an invitation to attend. But he has remained friendly with the Princess's mother, Princess Grace, and it was she who was present in March 1981 at Lady Diana's official 'launch' as fiancée of Prince Charles.

At this point it is worth recording the romance that never was, the affair that Prince Charles is said to have had with Princess Marie-Astrid of Luxembourg. But there never was a chance of marriage between them for two major reasons: first, they didn't know each other, except very vaguely, and secondly she was a Roman Catholic, which was even more significant.

The story, except for brief and infrequent mumblings, did not 'take off' until June 1977, in the middle of Royal Ascot week. Then, almost out of the blue, the *Daily Express* announced 'exclusively' that Prince Charles was to marry Marie-Astrid and the word 'Official' was added to the end of the headline.

At first the Prince reacted with enormous amusement. Breakfast time at Windsor Castle that morning was, I am told, an occasion of great merriment. As Prince Charles entered the breakfast room the Castle guests, already assembled, bowed in subservient fashion, offering their 'congratulations' on his betrothal. The conversation continued in this vein for some time, but eventually the mood turned much more serious and it was agreed that the one thing that stopped it all being a joke was the use of the word 'official'.

Following extensive inquiries over the next day or two, I was told that the 'extent of their relationship' was that the Prince, after a check had been made in the Buckingham Palace filing system, admitted he had met Princess Marie-Astrid on three occasions. But, not very flatteringly, he couldn't actually remember ever doing so.

While all this was going on, a posse of journalists was sent to Luxembourg to 'sort out the truth'. This minute principality, most famous for its commercial radio station, was turned into a circus ring for the best part of a week as a great deal of 'digging' went forward. I wasn't surprised at the result of all this. Absolutely nothing newsworthy came out of Luxembourg during these seven days. I maintained then, and have done so ever since, that there never was a romance.

On the same afternoon of the *Daily Express* story I was given permission to approach Prince Charles before a game of polo at Smith's Lawn, Windsor, to ask him to sort the whole business out. In a five-minute interview, which was without precedent, I was assured by Prince Charles that there was absolutely no truth at all in the story of an imminent engagement.

He went on: 'I have only just left the Navy [it had happened the previous December] and I am in no hurry to marry.' Looking rather stern and very serious he continued: 'I have not met the woman I want to marry and there is no question of any engagement or marriage in the next few months.'

On the subject of Princesss Marie-Astrid herself, the Prince was most concerned.

'I feel desperately sorry for her. She has been put in an impossible position because of this totally unfounded publicity. She did not court it and yet she finds herself in the position of having to deny a

. . . and Princess Marie-Astrid

. . . and Susan George

'when will I see you again?'

romance that doesn't exist.'

To try to quell the story on an even wider level, Prince Charles authorized the Queen's then press secretary, Mr Ronald Allison, to issue a denial of any wedding plans. The statement, put out at midnight, said: 'I am authorized by the Prince of Wales to make the following statement. "There is no truth at all in the report that there is to be an announcement of an engagement of the Prince of Wales to Princess Marie-Astrid of Luxembourg".'

The following day another statement was issued: 'They are not getting engaged this Monday, next Monday, the Monday after, or any other Monday, Tuesday, Wednesday or Thursday. They do not know each other and people who do not know each other do not get engaged. The Royal Family do not go in for arranged marriages. If the Prince and Princess Marie-Astrid have met at all then it has been briefly at official functions.'

But still, many knowledgeable students of this subject continued firmly to believe that the two knew each other a lot better than had ever been officially admitted.

In November 1976, for instance, Tony Holden reported a lunch at Laeken Palace in Brussels, at which Prince Charles, Prince Philip, King Baudouin and Queen Fabiola of the Belgians were present. Also at the lunch were the Belgian primate, Cardinal Joseph Suenens, and Bishop Jean Hengen, head of the Luxembourg Church. Tony Holden commented: 'Few believe Buckingham Palace's denial that she too [Princess Marie-Astrid who, with her sister, Margaretha, was at that time living at Laeken Palace] was at the lunch.'

There was much talk of comings and goings between the Foreign Office, Church officials and senior members of the Vatican to 'find a way out'. The rumours and innuendo continued, with the Queen allegedly saying, 'I find her enchanting.' But despite all this, nothing ever happened. Or rather nothing happened until an uncharacteristically blunt message was released by the Queen's press secretary, Michael Shea, at the end of 1980. In answer to a question from a Press Association reporter, Mr Shea – clearly after getting approval from the Prince himself – stated 'There has never been any plan for the two to marry.' He added, They have not even met in recent years.' The statement, Mr Shea said, was being put out 'because of recent events', and it effectively ended four days of speculation over whether the Act of Settlement of 1701 was about to be altered. Under this Act, the Prince could not marry a Roman Catholic and at the same time remain heir to the throne. The great dream that these two might one day overcome religious problems and get married was thus over forever. The way was left clear for Lady Diana to continue to be courted without further distraction.

As the Prince approached his thirtieth birthday – the time which he had said was a good age to get married – his attentions were turned increasingly towards the showbusiness set. No mean actor himself, while at school and university he had always been fascinated by showbiz talk and people, and one actress in particular who took his fancy at this time was Susan George. She had made her name as the rape victim in the X-rated film *Straw Dogs*.

There have been many references to the Prince's infatuation for Susan. It has been said he found her attractive and amusing. It has been said she was his favourite fantasy. Maybe she was, but she was also a lot more. Delectable Susan George was total reality for Prince Charles.

Susan, blonde, and one of the most sexually appealing actresses in Britain, first got to know Prince Charles at his thirtieth birthday party at Buckingham Palace on 14 November 1978, having received an invitation 'out of the blue.' The Prince later explained he had so enjoyed her film that he just wanted to meet her. Susan was stunned, but readily accepted. During that evening, and as his favourite group, the Three Degrees, sang 'When will I see you again?' the Prince took Susan's telephone number.

A few days later he called her home in Wraysbury, Buckinghamshire. Susan's maid, Doris, took the call. Not knowing who was on the end of the phone, and not asking, Doris explained that Susan was with her mum – just up the road. She gave 'the caller' the appropriate telephone number. A few moments later, the phone rang there too and Susan was handed the receiver by her mother, who similarly hadn't bothered to ask who was calling. With a shriek, Susan discovered that the person at the end of the line was HRH himself.

Susan laughed unbelievingly. 'How did you find out I was here?'

Prince Charles explained that he had got the number from Doris, and that he was ringing to invite her to dinner.

Susan didn't hesitate for a moment. She said: 'I'd love to come.'

A couple of days later a car was sent to collect her at her home, Green Tiles, and she was grandly whisked to a secret address in St James's, near the famous wine merchants, Berry Bros. As she was ushered into the flat, she found the Prince waiting for her and the dinner table laid out in formal style with two candles romantically burning. 'It looked beautiful and enchanting,' she has said of her first impression that evening.

They had a drink and then sat down to dinner, waited on by a formally dressed servant. Susan stayed nearly all night. She did not get home until 7 a.m. the following day.

One week later, exactly the same thing happened. A car picked her up and took her to the same apartment. Susan has since said that both evenings were 'wonderful'. She has also commented that the Prince was 'very romantic and loving'.

The Prince certainly took Susan out on one other occasion: when he escorted her to the theatre to see Barry Humphries in his famous role of Dame Edna Everage. They were spotted afterwards, going back to Buckingham Palace, where she had dinner with him.

Susan has never talked about that evening in his private apartment on the second floor overlooking St James's Park and the Mall. But that night they were seen by a press photographer at the theatre, and their meetings ended almost immediately. Both agreed that, if they were seen together in public more than once, their relationship would be considered a romance. It was something that could never be.

Susan has retained her friendship with the Prince, and they still meet occasionally, but never again will it be when they are alone or in that same apartment. Susan and her present live-in lover, Derek Webster, have since been invited to Windsor Castle and were reported as having attended the Queen Mother's eightieth birthday ball there during the 1980 Royal Ascot week.

Astounding offers of money – including a figure approaching £500,000 from one Fleet Street newspaper alone – to 'reveal all' have never tempted Susan George to talk publicly about her affair with Prince Charles. Once she nearly weakened, but she soon changed her mind, and the innermost secrets of what went on those nights will remain with just the two of them for ever.

Prince Charles's fascination for blondes from the world of show business has come out on other occasions. He is certainly remembered for having shown more than a passing interest in the delicious Lynsey de Paul one evening two or three years ago. The two met at a charity dinner party at the Ritz hotel in Piccadilly.

Fellow guests that night sat entranced as the Prince grew more and more friendly towards Lynsey, clearly bowled over by the diminutive singer's looks and bubbly personality. At the dinner table, Lynsey was sitting opposite Prince Charles who, naturally, was in the middle. As the meal continued to be served, Lynsey became aware of the Prince's foot touching hers. By the time the coffee was on the table, she felt him stroking her knee. The suspense was unbearable. Exciting in one way, nerve-wracking in another. She certainly couldn't say anything.

Someone who was present that night told me: 'It was almost embarrassing the way the Prince was flirting with Lynsey. It was incredibly obvious that he found her attractive and he didn't mind showing his affections. I think Lynsey enjoyed the attention he gave her, but it is a bit hard to deny the heir to the throne.'

At the conclusion of the evening the Prince made no further amorous move towards Lynsey. In fact, they both ended up having a sing-song with some of the other guests, including Elton John and Gary Glitter. The Prince and Lynsey, once a permanent fixture in the life of American actor James Coburn, have met since this night, but nothing was said. Both viewed what had happened as an amusing diversion.

The most attractive girl to be 'linked' with Prince Charles in the mid-1970s was Davina Sheffield, whose name the Scots rather charmingly pronounce 'Diviner'. She spent several week-ends at Balmoral in 1976 with HRH, and on one memorable occasion rode in a pony and trap alongside the Prince while the two were staying at Windsor.

Davina, with long blonde hair, like so many of the Prince's ladies, and always with a smile on her lips, was quite strongly tipped to be the one to get her Prince down the aisle. But her hopes were dashed when news of her friendship with Old Harrovian James Beard, came to light including the fact that she and James, a powerboat racer, had once shared a cottage.

It was perfectly all right for the Prince to have discreet liaisons wherever possible, but another matter for any of his girl friends to have done the same.

It was only one of two tragic blows to hit Davina at around this time. The other was that Davina's mother was murdered by raiders who overpowered her while ransacking her Oxfordshire home. Davina, who had, in the middle of her romance with Prince Charles, dramatically gone off to work with orphans in Saigon, returned after having news of the tragedy.

She turned to Prince Charles for comfort, and he was happy to supply it. They weekended in Balmoral again, and then, that autumn, Davina, with a few friends, rented a house in the beautiful and lonely Outer Hebridean island of South Uist (where Hercules the Bear recently went on the loose and got himself into the news).

It was wrongly reported at the beginning of the week that the Prince was going to join Davina in a 'love nest' on the island. I flew there to discover what was going on, and spent a very pleasant week waiting for the Prince to arrive. He never did, but this was not a fact to put Fleet Street off wanting to get any scrap of information going. So

. . . and Lynsey de Paul

when Davina finally returned to Heathrow airport, via Glasgow, half the plane down to London from Scotland was full of journalists, myself included.

Despite continuous denials that there was to be any engagement announcement, another fifty or so photographers were awaiting our arrival at Heathrow. There was total chaos and confusion as the plane landed.

Davina, always so cool, sophisticated and elegant, emerged with her head held high and walked towards the terminal. She so nearly made the last bit of the journey with dignity. Only in the final few strides did she crack as a voice from the crowd suddenly shouted: 'When are you going to marry Charlie, then?'

Davina burst into tears and headed straight for the ladies, where she stayed for nearly two hours, sobbing for most of the time. She finally left with a police escort.

It was a harrowing occasion all round, and nobody came out of the day with much credit. Davina later told a friend it had been one of the most terrible moments of her life.

The Prince did continue to see Davina after this – and until this day they still speak to each other by telephone – but the heat of their passion was never again so intense.

One more amusing incident in the same year had involved Davina being caught in the nude by a beach guard in Devon. It happened after the Prince and Davina had been surfing on a secluded beach at Bantham, near Kingsbridge, a place he had discovered while at Dartmouth Royal Naval College.

After the swim, Davina went to the men's changing room by mistake. She was standing completely starkers when a muscular life-saver, Ray Atkinson, walked in on her. Davina said nothing about the incident to the Prince, but Ray couldn't keep quiet. And the story appeared in the newspapers.

'It was a great sight,' said Ray, 'but very unexpected. She didn't bat an eyelid.'

With an aplomb like that, who is to say that Davina wouldn't have made an excellent Queen? But Davina has never married anybody.

. . . and Davina Sheffield

The girl who replaced Davina at the side of Prince Charles was Lady Sarah Spencer, Lady Diana's delightful red-haired elder sister. Sarah, who had the slimmer's disease, anorexia nervosa, at the beginning of her friendship with the Prince, always insisted that their relationship was platonic. But they were very good friends, and they remain so.

Sarah, whose godmother is the Queen Mother, always said that her meeting with the Prince in June 1977 (they did not know each other as children, and this was the first time they ever met) had nothing to do with her starting to recover from anorexia. But the fact remains that within a month and a half of this meeting Sarah elected to go into hospital for treatment and six months later was 'very much better'.

Her first public appearance with Prince Charles took place at Royal Ascot in the week of the Marie-Astrid and *Daily Express* business. Sarah was staying at Windsor Castle as part of the Queen's house party. 'I was invited right out of the blue,' she told me soon afterwards. 'Although my family had a house next door to Sandringham, and the Royal Family and mine had known each other for years, I had never met Prince Charles until that week.'

But, having done so, the two became constant companions, with Sarah frequently travelling to Smith's Lawn to watch the Prince play polo. Inevitably there was talk of love between the two, and suggestions that one day there might even be marriage. But, apart from admitting to me that she was very fond of Prince Charles and that he made her laugh a lot, Sarah has always maintained that she was not in love with him.

Speculation about their future grew even stronger the following February 1978, when Lady Sarah joined the Prince for a skiing holiday in Klosters, Switzerland. But, after spending the best part of two weeks together under the same chalet roof, Sarah maintained her 'just good friends' routine. In fact, she kept to the theme so well that Prince Charles's considerable ego where women are concerned took quite a dent.

When I took Sarah to lunch one day, she began to tell me what she thought of the Prince.

'He is fabulous as a person, but I am not in love with him,' she said. 'He is a romantic who falls in love easily. But I can assure you that

. . . and Lady Sarah Spencer

if there were to be any engagement between Prince Charles and myself, it would have happened by now.

'I am a whirlwind sort of lady as opposed to a person who goes in for long, slow-developing courtships. Of course, the Prince and I are great friends, but I was with him in Switzerland because of my skiing ability.

(In fact, Sarah isn't nearly as good a skier as Diana, and the Prince used to tease her about holding them all up on the ski slopes.)

'Our relationship is totally platonic. I do not believe that Prince Charles wants to marry yet. He has still not met the person he wants to marry. I think of him as the big brother I never had.'

Then,.to sever the idea of their particular 'romance' for ever, Sarah added: 'I wouldn't marry anyone I didn't love, whether it was the dustman or the King of England. If he asked me I would turn him down.'

There have been many things said about this interview: that it was tricked out of Lady Sarah, that it went into a women's magazine without her knowledge, that it ended her friendship with Prince Charles, that it offended him.

The truth is that Sarah agreed to talk to me at her South Kensington home in front of two witnesses, that she knew it was for *Woman's Own* magazine, that it did not end her friendship with the Prince and that, yes, he was a bit upset at what she had said.

Within minutes of speaking to me Sarah telephoned to tell the Prince what she had done. He was not over-pleased at her indiscretion but said it didn't sound as if any real damage had been done. He did, however, feel a bit peeved that Sarah had quite so publicly told the world she was not in love with him. It was not the sort of thing to do anybody's reputation any good, particularly the reputation of a lover of women like Prince Charles.

Any lingering annoyance the Prince might have carried for Sarah must by now have evaporated. After all, he is going to have to spend the rest of his life as her brother-in-law!

Throughout all those years of romancing, flirting and wooing almost countless members of the opposite sex, one girl above all others remained a constant factor in the life of Prince Charles. This was Lady Jane Wellesley, the dark-haired daughter of the Duke of Wellington. And she, I have aways been told, was the first girl with whom the Prince really fell in love. One of their mutual friends has said to me: 'I always thought they would marry, but the pressure on them at the time [in 1974] was so great it ended their romance.'

I have never felt any doubt that if Prince Charles and Jane had had their 1973-4 'affair' six years later, then the two would have been married. Jane was in every way suitable to become Princess of Wales. She was pretty, intelligent, bright and well versed in the ways of court life, though not a member of the Royal Family. She also had the backing of the Queen and Prince Philip who, like nearly everybody else, thought Jane a splendid girl.

It was all a question of too much, too soon; and then, having decided that they should wait, both started to draw away from actually becoming engaged. Prince Charles had his naval career to consider, while Jane, ironically, had a burning desire to succeed in journalism – the very thing that caused them so much heartache during the early days of their courtship.

The 'climax' of their feeling for each other reached a peak in

. . . and Lady Jane Wellesley

1973, soon after they had holidayed together in Molino de Rey, the Duke of Wellington's 30,000-acre estate near Granada in southern Spain. I was assigned to that particular story, and when I talked to Jane as we both came through customs at Heathrow, she was ecstatic at the holiday they had both enjoyed together.

But she was only twenty-three at the time, and she was scared. It is a pity that the two were not left alone by the press for a few months to 'sort themselves out'. But they weren't and the chemistry between them started to evaporate. It didn't disappear completely until quite recently, and certainly in all the years between 1974 and the Prince's engagement in February 1981 they never lost touch with each other.

Jane was one of those rare girls who grew up with the Prince, attended parties with him when they were both young, and continued to mix with him in adulthood. In some ways, they almost knew each other too well. In 1977 there was further talk that marriage between them might be on again. She spent a week-end at Balmoral and travelled over to Scone Palace with Prince Charles to watch him play polo. She was close to tears that day since she had wanted to say good-bye properly when returning to London. But, because of the barage of press attention, she had to drift sadly away.

Since then Jane has grown rather more arty and independent while pursuing a career at the BBC. She shocked many people by becoming Mother of the Chapel (head of her union branch) when she worked on the *Radio Times*. But she enjoys her independence and has often told friends: 'I couldn't, just couldn't,give everything up to become his wife.'

In a flash of temper on another occasion when asked if there was to be an engagement, she said: 'Do you honestly believe I want to be the Queen?'

But she has always been happy and proud to be the Prince's friend, and will continue to do anything to help when she is asked. At the ball given before their separation by the Earl and Countess of Pembroke at their fabulous Wiltshire home, Wilton House, the Prince spent much of the evening dancing with Jane, even though the Prince was ostensibly there with his then girl friend, Sabrina Guinness. One clumsy guest spilt wine over Prince Charles and his dinner jacket. Jane rushed forward, took the handkerchief from his pocket and carefully cleaned him down. It was a touching moment.

But that original spark was by then missing for both of them, and one can only hope that Jane now finds somebody else with whom she too can settle down. She will always receive the Prince's best wishes.

If Lord Mountbatten had had his way, the Prince of Wales would have married Lady Amanda Knatchbull. It was the Earl's great dream before his assassination that HRH would marry one of his grand-daughters. And the one he favoured by far was Lady Amanda.

Out of respect for his adored 'Uncle Dickie', the Prince did everything he could to create a state whereby he might just fall in love with her. He would spend week-ends with her, he would talk to her for hours when she was a guest at Sandringham or Balmoral. He went on holiday to the tiny island of Eleutherea, where Amanda's parents had a home, and he would enjoy skiing and lying on a beach with her. They adored each other. But only as friends, never as potential husband and wife. And, at the end of 1980, they agreed that marriage could never happen between them.

They remain pals and will do so always.

. . . and Amanda Knatchbull

One of the most curious 'girl friends' ever attributed to Prince Charles was Jane Ward, a lively, happy-go-lucky blonde divorcee who got to know the Prince through being the assistant manager at the Guards Polo Club at Windsor. During the summer of 1979, their friendship, through a mixture of intrigue and jealousy, became the talk of many people. They would be spotted, laughing and chatting together, clearly enjoying each other's company.

Wrongly, word started to spread that they were more than just good friends, and one day Jane got wind that the *Daily Express* gossip columnist, William Hickey, was to chronicle their activities, adding that the Queen was 'concerned' about the relationship. To correct this story, Jane gave an interview to two journalists, one of whom was myself, explaining that any suggestion of a romance was 'laughable'. As a result of a misunderstanding, Jane was shocked the following day to discover that everything she had said was in banner headlines. Her world went upside down and she couldn't get on the phone fast enough to apologize to Prince Charles. He wasn't at Buckingham Palace to receive her call.

. . . and Jane Ward

Things only went from bad to worse for poor Jane. As if the first story wasn't embarrassing enough, there was more misery to come when, in a follow-up, Jane was reported as being told to 'get lost' by the Prince's detective, John MacLean. This was said to have happened when she turned up at a game of polo at Lord Cowdray's ground at Midhurst in which Prince Charles was playing. No such 'brush-off' was ever given. In fact, the truth was quite the contrary. John, passing on 'concern' from the Prince, was purely telling Jane not to worry.

Indeed, earlier that day, and before the press had arrived at Midhurst, the Prince had personally told Jane that he was not worried. He went so far as to say to her: 'I won't suffer, but I am afraid you will.' Unfortunately, Jane chose to leave the Midhurst ground immediately after John MacLean had spoken to her, leaving reporters to put two and two together – quite inaccurately.

Jane has never publicly explained what her feelings were at this time, but I understand that, while the Prince had felt she might have been a bit silly and naive in talking at all, he was never cross with her. They have met since while out hunting (on his birthday in November 1979), and they have talked on the telephone. The Prince has shown only concern for Jane. His message to her is always the same: 'I am so sorry this happened, but don't worry.'

Jane, for her part, now only feels upset that she 'lost a real friend' and has regrets that 'her family became embroiled in the whole issue'. My own feeling is that the Prince lost a friend too. Jane was one of the few people that the Prince has ever met who would give him a straight answer to a straight question.

It was in 1979 – in May – that the Prince admitted publicly that he was finally seriously thinking of settling down. He told the Association of Headteachers that he had received a postcard saying: 'What you need is a good wife.'

'I am sure that is exactly what I do need,' he said in a speech, half serious and half humorous. But it was at last an indication that marriage was beginning to occupy a large slice of his thoughts.

It was at about this time, too, that he started dating Sabrina Guinness of the brewery family. There was much controversy about the relationship between Charles and Sabrina, but there never was a chance that there could be marriage between them. However hard Sabrina

. . . and Sabrina Guinness

tried to change her image, she was thought of as having a past, and in the public's mind this excluded her from being a suitable choice.

Sabrina was fun and she enjoyed life, parties and gadding about with famous people. Far too much so, said many. Her 'past' included friendships with Tatum O'Neal; the self-confessed bisexual singer, David Bowie; the creator of the television series, *The Likely Lads* and *Porridge*, Ian La Frenais; Mick Jagger; Rod Stewart and the Oscar-winning womanizer, Jack Nicholson.

Pretty blonde Sabrina tried to change all that. She started to shed her image of a trendy star-chaser. She thought that, however good pop idols and film stars might be for her, the Prince of Wales was even better. She started involving herself in charity fund-raising occasions, and taking wholesome trips to the country at week-ends.

She played down her romance with Prince Charles, as when she told me: 'Please don't try to marry us off. Don't put pressures on us.'

But, all the time, she was hoping something would come of their relationship. She travelled to Balmoral under a false name. She stopped wearing the wrong sort of clothes. As a friend said at the time: 'She has become terribly county. She used to wear outrageous clothes. Now she is into plain, tweedy outfits. She is also much more subdued that she was. I think she is desperately trying to get away from the image she had in the past of mixing with movie people, pop singers and people on the fringe of the drug-taking scene.'

...until, after Sabrina, Charles began to think it really was time to settle down, after all.

However serious Sabrina was about achieving all this, she failed. On the day of the engagement between Diana and Charles, Sabrina was asked what she thought about it. Although in one of her favourite nightspots, Tokyo Joe's, run by Dai Llewellyn, Sabrina could barely raise a smile. Eventually she managed to whisper: 'I wish them luck.'

Thus Prince Charles arrived eventually at his final fling before moving into the gentle arms of Lady Diana for ever. His affair with the fiery Anna Wallace – known to her friends as 'Whiplash Wallace' – was dramatic, tempestuous, very sensuous and, at times, incredibly passionate.

During their relationship, which lasted from November 1979 until July 1980, the Prince asked Anna to become his wife. Anna said no. She knew only too well that many people would never accept her as Prince Charles's bride. She admitted to having had lovers in the past, she admitted to having too wilful a nature ever to become a member of the Royal Family, she admitted she was wrong for Prince Charles. She also knew that the Queen wasn't at all keen about her. And that Fleet Street hardly viewed her with much love and warmth.

When Prince Charles asked her to marry him, she was thrown right back on her heels. She knew she couldn't accept. It would have been impossible, and she rang her former employer, the fabulously rich Iranian socialite, Homayoun Mazandi, to ask what she should do.

'It just won't work,' she stated.

Homayoun who had, before Anna, employed Marie-Christine von Reibnitz as her private secretary prior to her marriage to Prince Michael of Kent, didn't know what to say.

Prince Charles, despite being rejected, remained besotted with Anna. He didn't care that the gossip columist, Nigel Dempster, had written about two of her previous lovers.

'Don't give me any answer at the moment,' he told her. 'Let's both think about it.'

He took her on a secret holiday to Balmoral in Scotland in May 1980. Instead of fishing from morning until dusk, as he usually does, I found him lying on a rug on the river bank with Anna. It was right out of character, certainly at that time of the day. He grew more angry than I have ever known him when I followed them along the river Dee with

Ken Lennox, trying to get pictures. He even authorized his friend Lord Tony Tryon to shout a four-letter word across the river 'suggesting' we go away.

He encouraged Anna, with the aid of the binoculars, to pin-point Ken Lennox and myself as his detective, Jim McMaster, tried to find out where we were hiding across the river later that same day.

Anna could do almost anything, and it would be approved of by Prince Charles. But in the end, the intensity of it all became too much and, predictably, there was an explosion. For the first time in his life Prince Charles was 'dropped' – and loudly – by one of his girl friends. The end took place over two long, hot uncomfortable nights.

It began at the eightieth birthday ball given in honour of the Queen Mother at Windsor Castle during Royal Ascot week in the middle of June 1980. With many important guests at the dance, the Prince felt he should spend his time with them. Anna didn't object to this. She just felt that she shouldn't be completely left out of what was happening. And she told him so. She told HRH in a loud voice: 'Don't ever ignore me like that again. I've never been treated so badly in my life.'

As the blood drained from Prince Charles's face and he tried to come up with a suitable answer, Anna went on: 'No one treats me like that – not even you'.

Soon after this came part two of the final act. This time the scene had switched to Stowell Park, the fabulous Gloucestershire estate of Lord Vestey who was holding a polo ball. With Prince Charles trying to show who was the boss, Anna watched with increasing fury as her lover had dance after dance with his favourite married woman, Camilla Parker-Bowles. It went on all evening. Not even Lady Vestey – Kate to her friends – was asked to dance, and she was the Prince's hostess.

Anna became more and more angry as she was ignored. In the end she borrowed Kate's BMW car and drove back to London. And she and the Prince never had tender or civil words for each other from that day on.

The story was circulated in London society that HRH had sent emissaries to persuade Anna to speak to him so he could explain. But she wouldn't, and with almost unseemly haste was soon engaged and married to Johnny Hesketh, younger brother of Lord Hesketh.

It had been a traumatic experience for Prince Charles, and only the gentleness and affection of Lady Diana Spencer helped him to recover from the shock as quickly as he did. He had been made to realize that the playing around really should stop. He had had a fabulous run, but now he was thirty-two and had a duty to find a wife.

Diana was the ideal person. He swore that the one big difference with this romance was that there would be nowhere near the usual amount of publicity. To help him achieve his aim, Prince Charles used a house he had bought secretly in the Campden Hill area near Notting Hill Gate in the early part of 1980.

Locals in this select part of West London rarely saw him in the area and were left guessing as to the precise address. Some said it was a terraced house in Campden Street. Others that it was the penthouse in Kensington Heights, an elegant block of modern flats opposite the Windsor Castle pub.

What was important was that the scheme was successful. His love nest, where he could woo Diana on occasions, was never discovered until after the engagement announcement. And by then the place had been put up for sale and quietly disposed of.

Photographic Credits

Camera Press Ltd: see pages 12, 13, 14, 31, 47 (left), 110 (top), 111 (middle), 119 (top)
Arthur Edwards: 106 (right)
London Express: 105, 106 (left), 109 (top), 110 (bottom), 111 (top left), 112
Fox Photos Ltd: 6, 8, 11, 15, 26, 32, 33, 34, 44, 104
Tim Graham: 16, 19, 20 (top), 21, 23, 24, 28, 29, 35, 36, 37, 41, 42, 43, 48, 50, 53, 55, 57, 58, 59, 61, 62, 66, 67, 73, 80, 83, 84, 87, 88, 89, 94, 96, 97, 101, 119 (bottom), 122, 123, 126
Anwar Hussein: 46, 47 (right top & bottom), 100, 104, 111 (right), 113 (bottom right), 114, 121, 124
Keystone Press Agency Ltd: 90
Desmond O'Neill: 108
Photographers International Ltd: 20 (bottom), 77, 111 (bottom), 115, 120, 125
Press Association: 113 (top)
Rex Features Ltd: 107 (bottom)
Universal Pictorial Press & Agency Ltd: 109 (bottom), 118
Richard Young: 107 (top)
Main cover photo: Photographers International
Cover montage photographs courtesy of: (left to right) Camera Press, Tim Graham, Anwar Hussein, Universal Pictorial Press & Agency Ltd., Rex Features Ltd., Photographers International Ltd., Richard Young